The Italian Risorgimento

MARTIN CLARK

LONGMAN
LONDON AND NEW YORK

Addison Wesley Longman Limited
Edinburgh Gate
Harlow, Essex CM20 2JE
England

and Associated Companies throughout the world.

*Published in the United States of America
by Addison Wesley Longman Inc., New York*

First published 1998

ISBN 0 582 003539

British Library Cataloguing-in-Publication Data

A catalogue record for this book is
available from the British Library

Library of Congress Cataloging-in-Publication Data

Clark, Martin, 1938–
    The Italian Risorgimento / Martin Clark.
        p. cm. — (Seminar studies in history)
    Includes bibliographical references and index.
    ISBN 0-582-00353-9
    1. Italy—History—1815–1870. I. Title. II. Series.
DG552.C54 1998
945'. 083—dc21   97–42541
                                                          CIP
                                                          AC

Set by 7 in 10/12 Sabon
Printed in Malaysia by VVP

CONTENTS

AN INTRODUCTION TO THE SERIES

Such is the pace of historical enquiry in the modern world that there is an ever-widening gap between the specialist article or monograph, incorporating the results of current research, and general surveys, which inevitably become out of date. *Seminar Studies in History* are designed to bridge this gap. The series was founded by Patrick Richardson in 1966 and his aim was to cover major themes in British, European and World history. Between 1980 and 1996 Roger Lockyer continued his work, before handing the editorship over to Clive Emsley and Gordon Martel. Clive Emsley is Professor of History at the Open University, while Gordon Martel is Professor of International History at the University of Northern British Columbia, Canada and Senior Research Fellow at De Montfort University.

All the books are written by experts in their field who are not only familiar with the latest research but have often contributed to it. They are frequently revised, in order to take account of new information and interpretations. They provide a selection of documents to illustrate major themes and provoke discussion, and also a guide to further reading. The aim of *Seminar Studies* is to clarify complex issues without over-simplifying them, and to stimulate readers into deepening their knowledge and understanding of major themes and topics.

NOTE ON REFERENCING SYSTEM

Readers should note that numbers in square brackets [5] refer them to the corresponding entry in the Bibliography at the end of the book (specific page numbers are given in italics). A number in square brackets preceded by *Doc.* [*Doc.* 5] refers readers to the corresponding item in the Documents section which follows the main text. Words and abbreviations asterisked at first occurrence are defined in the Glossary.

LIST OF MAPS

ACKNOWLEDGEMENTS

Many people have helped me prepare this book. I should like, in particular, to thank Denis Mack Smith, for first arousing my interest in Risorgimento history. I should also like to thank Roger Lockyer who invited me to write the book. I am also grateful to all the helpful library staff of the Edinburgh University Library, the National Library of Scotland, and the Italian National Libraries in Florence and Rome.

PART ONE: THE BACKGROUND

1 INTRODUCTION

The Italian word *risorgimento* means 'revival', or 'resurrection' (of the dead). In the early- and mid-nineteenth century, it also meant a broad cultural, social and economic 'revival', when Italy emerged from the (allegedly) stagnant provincialism of previous centuries. In addition, it meant the period when foreign rulers were expelled from the Italian peninsula, and when the various Italian States were 'unified' into a single Kingdom of Italy in 1861. It has often been argued that these two aspects, the cultural and the political, were connected via the demand for 'liberty'. Rapid cultural changes meant a better-educated people, demanding greater freedoms – not only to trade or to move abroad, but also to have free speech, a free press, free association, even the vote and a say in policy-making; but most Italian states would not or could not grant these concessions. Hence people came to demand a new political regime, one which would guarantee liberty.

Independence, unification, and liberty – these were to be the three grand political themes of the Risorgimento. However, they were not necessarily connected. Independence from foreign rule might well have been achieved without unification, and indeed until at least the mid-1850s most patriotic Italians assumed that it would be. Similarly, there was no guarantee that the unified Italian state after 1861 would be more 'liberal' than at least some of its predecessors. Nonetheless, between 1859–61 all three were, to all appearances, achieved quite suddenly, indeed miraculously, after an epic, heroic expedition to win Sicily, led by the greatest and noblest of Italian soldiers, Giuseppe Garibaldi. This new kingdom did guarantee liberty, at least until the Fascist takeover in the 1920s. It is not surprising, then, that later generations of Italians have looked back to the Risorgimento as a glorious period. Socially and ideologically, it embodied the triumph of economic modernity and of rational thought over traditional prejudice and clerical obscurantism; politically, it ensured constitutional liberty, national independence and even Great Power status.

This patriotic 'Whig' view, although still surprisingly entrenched, is not really tenable. To begin with, it is too 'teleological': it assumes the process was virtually inevitable. In fact, Italian unification was, like most historical events, the result of a complex series of unforeseeable 'accidents'. The eventual outcome had not been predicted even by the leading personalities involved, nor was it welcome to most of them. Moreover, the patriotic view assumes that Italian nationhood already existed, just waiting to be embodied in national institutions. But Italy, as Metternich famously remarked in 1847, was simply a 'geographical expression'. Her inhabitants were mostly peasants who spoke only their local dialect. The language of Dante and Machiavelli, although written by the literate few, was spoken by about 2.5 per cent of the population, most of them in Tuscany or Rome. Even in the towns people's horizons were not 'national', nor even regional; they were municipal. The rivalry between nearby cities had deep historical roots and was still strongly felt. Only a tiny educated minority felt 'Italian' and celebrated Italy's glorious past; but they were too few to matter much. By the 1840s such men – for the most part professors, lawyers, or journalists – were indeed proclaiming an intellectual and cultural programme of 'revival', and demanding civil liberties and constitutional government, but most members of the various municipal, political, landowning and commercial elites were still unimpressed. Moreover, most of these writers and intellectuals advocated 'independence' from foreign rule, but not 'unity': a single Italian state seemed, even to them, not only impossible but undesirable. Italy, they thought, should ideally become a confederation of independent states, all enjoying constitutional liberties, but all different and respectful of varying local conditions: 'unification' yes, but not 'unity'. Even Pope Pius IX, elected in 1846, could support this programme for a time, and many people wanted him to lead it. In short, the 'patriotic' interpretation is mistaken, if only because Italians were very divided and not anxious for national unity. Few Italians thought about the matter at all, and those few wanted confederalism, or at most federalism. And the Catholic Church, far from being necessarily an obscurantist obstacle to the whole movement, very nearly led it.

The patriotic 'Whig' interpretation also assumes that the actual outcome in 1861 – a united Italy, under a constitutional monarchy and parliamentary government – was the best of all possible results. This view has, of course, been criticized over the years, from both Left and Right. On the Left, Giuseppe Mazzini and his republican supporters rejected a regime run by a monarchical, militarist clique in league with a corrupt parliament elected by a tiny minority: the national revolution had, they argued, been undermined by Piedmontese aristocrats – often French-speaking, at that – who ruled for their own benefit, not that of the people. This view has often been repeated by radical historians, particularly those writing after the Resistance of 1943–5. Moreover, Communist historians have often echoed their mentor Antonio Gramsci in arguing that the Risorgimento was essentially a lost opportunity. There might have been a 'real' (social and economic) revolution in mid-nineteenth-century Italy, if only the republicans and 'democrats'* had allied with the peasantry, instead of supinely joining the 'moderate'* establishment. The Risorgimento was therefore a 'passive revolution', in which most Italians played no part, and in which governments and foreign Powers played the key role. That was why the 'liberal' rulers of united Italy after 1861 had little popular support. Revolts and rioting became commonplace, and governments for decades ruled by force, not consent. The 'liberal' regime was not liberal at all, just a small elite who were monopolising power and using it to impose alien values on the masses [40, 52].

On the Right, Catholic historians agreed with much of this. Analysing the impact of liberal government on the most observant Catholic regions like Venetia or Lombardy, they too stressed the peasants' sullen hostility to the new 'liberal' regime, and to the liberal imposition of 'lay' practices like compulsory state education and civil marriage. Catholic historians argued that after 1848 the essence of the Risorgimento was secularization. The state was exalted, in order to despoil the Church. The Pope was robbed of his Temporal Power*, the historic Papal States of central Italy; throughout Italy ecclesiastical lands and buildings were seized by the newly powerful. To attack the Church was to attack the people, especially the people's common resources and welfare provision. More 'lay' conservative historians have repeated this theme, with some variations. During the Fascist regime Gioacchino Volpe, for example, argued that the Risorgimento created an Italian state, but not a 'nation'; that great task still remained to be carried through, by the Fascists [114].

More recently, criticism of the Risorgimento has become more fundamental. The various pre-unification regimes have found their apologists. Bourbon rule in the Kingdom of Naples, for example, was, if not popular or efficient, at least considerably less unpopular and inefficient than nineteenth-century liberals like Gladstone (who called it 'the negation of God') supposed; even its prisons, famously denounced by Gladstone, were better than those of northern, progressive Piedmont [50, 87, i, *pp. 292–300*]. The Grand Duchy of

Tuscany, with its virtual free trade, its relaxed censorship and its highly-educated, tolerant duke, was certainly no tyranny; nor, for that matter, was Austrian-run Lombardy-Venetia, at least before 1848. True, some of the 'chattering classes' and professional men like lawyers and doctors were unhappy, but that was because they had little status and could not find jobs: the true weakness of the old regimes was not despotism or corruption, but failing to distribute enough patronage. Cynical historians, in short, tend to see the Risorgimento as an over-hyped media project, of no interest to most people but of great importance to those who thought they might benefit – journalists, lawyers and a few commercially-minded landowners, as well as the leading aristocrats and the royal dynasty of Piedmont. Unification itself, they argue, was mostly hype too. Italian society remained just as diverse and conflictual after 1861 as it had been before; and the new state was not really 'united' either. Parliamentary governments depended on local elites, who controlled the vote; these diverse elites therefore had to be allowed very considerable local power, and a large share in 'national' influence [102].

In recent years many historians have become more 'regionalist' in outlook. They stress that each region had its own traditions, which often survived unification. Southern historians, for example, show that the pre-1861 south was not a stagnant society, and that some of its peculiar institutions, like the huge *latifondo* estates, may have been an appropriate response to existing market forces and technology [89]. They also reject patronising northern concepts like 'backwardness' or 'modernization', and argue that it was unification, with its low tariffs and high taxes, that wrecked the southern economy. 'Unification', indeed, is in their view a misnomer. Italy was not 'unified'; northern Italy simply conquered the south. This provoked a bloody 'resistance' movement that lasted for years. Many contemporary northerners also regard annexing the south as a disastrous error. Gianfranco Miglio, for example, has argued that northern Italy would have been a far more prosperous and effective state on its own, without the economic burden of the south and the bureaucratic inertia of Rome; indeed, the Lombards would have been better off staying under the Austrians, rather than being controlled by the Piedmontese [86]. More subtly, the northerners argue that the united Italian state, never a true reality in any case, has now been superseded by the European Union and by economic 'globalization'. 'Unification' may have seemed progressive in the mid-nineteenth century, but 'nation-states' are now outmoded. At most, 'Italy' should be a 'postnationalist' term of reference. It may properly remain as one of many overlapping cultural identities, for those who choose to adopt it, but it should not necessarily have any political implications or institutions.

This brings me back to my original definition of the Risorgimento as a dual movement, both cultural and political. But how, if at all, were the 'cultural', ideological aspects linked to the political ones? Was it really via a demand for 'liberty', as I suggested earlier? The answer seems to be 'yes'; indeed, the people who mattered were more interested in 'liberty' than in 'unity' or even 'independence'. By the 1840s (not earlier) some, at least, of the pre-unification states did indeed have a 'legitimacy crisis': influential people stopped believing that their existing governments were entitled to rule them. Like the east European states of the 1980s, the Italian states of the 1840s and 1850s were undermined by an active dissident intelligentsia, aware of developments elsewhere and resentful of censorship and conformity at home. However, this was not true everywhere. It was much less true, if true at all, in Tuscany, Rome or the mainland south. And dissident intellectuals, however eminent or respected, could hardly have undermined established regimes on their own. For that, other factors were also necessary: unpopular changes in land tenure, grazing rights, guild structure and welfare; ineffective policing; administrative and judicial high-handedness. The old states duly obliged. People also needed greater awareness of the European world – easier travel, greater circulation of ideas and journals, heightened awareness of the economic possibilities opened by the new age of steam and the railway. Above all, perhaps, there had to be foreign approval. The Risorgimento had to be part of a 'European' movement, seeking to achieve in Italy what was already taken for granted in France or Britain. Arguably it was not a 'national' movement at all. Culturally, it was mostly 'European' in its ideas; politically, it was mostly triggered by European rivalries and wars, helped along by dynastic ambitions and a host of small-town, municipal grievances.

However, from 1848 onwards one Italian state did serve as a model. In that year King Charles Albert of Piedmont granted a 'liberal' constitution, guaranteeing civil liberties and a representative government responsible to an elected parliament. Piedmont thus became a haven for cultural dissidents; they could publish their writings fairly freely there. States elsewhere became more oppressive after 1848, but there was no 'legitimacy crisis' in Piedmont. On the contrary, Piedmont became a political beacon, the shining light of 'liberalism in one country'. Parliamentary government gave Piedmont its claim to be the only representative Italian state, a claim that became one to national leadership and – eventually – the right to impose its enlightened institutions elsewhere. Federalism, the solution preferred by most patriots before 1848, was abandoned in favour of the Piedmontese Constitution. The 'Whig' view may have been ludicrous earlier on, but it became rather more plausible in the 1850s.

Ultimately, of course, 'unification' was achieved not by propaganda nor by constitutions, but by war and by diplomatic alliances to make war. Piedmont had a respectable and disciplined army by Italian standards, but it was no match for the Austrians, as was proved in 1848–9. The Piedmontese Prime Minister, Camillo di Cavour, therefore had to secure foreign support for his ambitions. Foreign armies did most of the actual fighting for Italian unity, not only in 1859 but also in 1866 and 1870. In this sense, too, the Risorgimento was a 'European' movement. However, in most of these campaigns Italian volunteers and guerrilla fighters also played a vital part. It was Garibaldi's improvised expedition that conquered the South in 1860; it was the 'moderate' landowners and professional men of the 'National Society' who organised the vital insurrections in central Italy in 1859. Both these groups fought for 'Italy'. They illustrate well just how deeply the ideological, cultural movement of the previous decades had penetrated, and how 'cultural identity' could and did inspire political and military struggle. So the Risorgimento was not a 'state-with-an-army' annexing the states that had none; it was the 'state-with-modern-sounding-ideas' overwhelming those with apparently outmoded ones. The leaders of the Risorgimento may have been a small, unrepresentative minority of the Italian people, and the state they founded may have been 'liberal' largely in rhetoric and posture, but they did at least secure some degree of independence, and they did open up Italy to European trade and partnership. What they did not do was create an Italian 'nation'. If Italian identity is multiple now, it was no less multiple then.

PART TWO: DESCRIPTIVE ANALYSIS

2   THE IMPACT OF FRANCE

THE 'JACOBIN TRIENNIUM'

In May 1796 French troops led by Napoleon Bonaparte invaded Italy. Within the next three years, Napoleon founded a series of short-lived, French-dominated republics. The Cisalpine Republic ruled Lombardy and much of northern Italy, previously ruled by the Austrians; the Ligurian Republic replaced the old Republic of Genoa. Piedmont, known officially until 1861 as the 'Kingdom of Sardinia', was permitted to retain its monarchy and its formal independence, but the French took over the king's territories in Savoy and Nice. In February 1798 the French also ended papal rule in Rome, and founded the Roman Republic; in December they finally occupied Piedmont; in January 1799 it was the turn of Naples (the 'Parthenopean Republic'), and in March of Tuscany. The ancient Republic of Venice, together with its hinterland, was abolished and came under Austrian rule in 1797. Apart from Venice, by early 1799 all mainland Italy was controlled by 'revolutionary' French authorities, who rapidly imposed French laws, administrative systems and attitudes to property.

Only the two large southern islands of Sardinia and Sicily remained free of French rule, although they, too, were influenced by French ideas. The French had, in fact, attempted to invade Sardinia as early as January 1793, but had been repulsed – the young Napoleon Bonaparte's first taste of real action was an inglorious defeat at La Maddalena. Sardinia continued to be ruled by the King of Piedmont, who resided on the island after being driven out of Turin; but it was protected by the British fleet. Indeed, Nelson sheltered his fleet at La Maddalena for about eighteen months, and urged that Britain should take the island over outright, as it had far better facilities than Malta. Sicily, too, soon became a British protectorate, and a refuge for the royal family of Naples.

Most of the 'French' republics on mainland Italy were more 'revolutionary' than, by 1798, was France itself. The French invaders claimed to have brought 'liberty', and a few Italians believed them. These *patrioti* were young, educated, usually from the urban middle classes or the lesser nobility – students, advocates, notaries, doctors, writers, some priests and friars, with a smattering of artisans and craftsmen. They were imbued with genuine enthusiasm for liberty, equality and progress; they detested the old royal despotisms, the old aristocratic privileges and the stranglehold of the established Catholic hierarchy. They were not numerous, but they could be relied on to fight for republican ideals, and they were excellent propagandists. On the other hand, they relied totally on the French. If the French withdrew their armies, the Republics would collapse, as everyone knew. Hence the *patrioti*, despite their name and despite their protestations, had no desire for Italian 'independence', at least for the foreseeable future.

But many of them did envisage Italian 'unification', i.e. a single Italian state ('a sister Republic'), at least in northern Italy. In September 1796 a famous essay competition was held in Milan, to determine what kind of government was best suited to Italy. The winner, Melchiorre Gioia, praised the French constitution of 1795 as a model and argued for Italian 'unity', with uniform legislation and taxes throughout the country (although he too probably thought in terms only of northern Italy). In practice, the *patrioti* had very little influence and had to be content with what the French had set up – not a single Italian republic, but a number of French-run states, with (paper) constitutions similar to that of France in 1795. They guaranteed such rights as a free press, free association, freedom of worship, and the equality of citizens before the law; and they had legislative assemblies, indirectly elected by the property-owners, with a separate executive and judiciary.

All this was usually a dead letter. The new Republics were certainly very different from their *ancien régime* predecessors, but they hardly lived up to democratic or Jacobin ideals. Their French governors were anxious mainly to maintain order and to extract food and taxes, to feed and pay for France's armies. The French, in fact, ruled via their army. Some of the local commanders simply looted whatever was valuable, including paintings from churches and monasteries. When the French needed competent local administrators, they turned not to the idealistic *patrioti* but to minor nobles and to the established middle class of lawyers and officials. Many of these men had been prominent as 'enlightened' reformers under the old regimes, and were perfectly willing to serve new masters. The French also relied, particularly for local government, on 'moderate' landowners, immersed in local family rivalries, who unfortunately had a distressing tendency to help themselves to public or Church lands, and who certainly had little time for traditional paternalism. For all these reasons some of the more radical *patrioti* soon became disillusioned. They founded clubs, or even secret societies like the *Società dei Raggi*, to press for greater social and political change, and if need be to organize further insurrections.

The high French land taxes and the constant food requisitions soon made the new regimes extremely unpopular, particularly with the peasantry. The French began to confiscate Church property: some huge estates were split up and sold off to new landowners. In addition, they tried to take poor relief, health care and, above all, education out of Church hands. In practice, this meant setting up workhouses for the able-bodied poor, and forcing children to receive 'patriotic' education at school instead of helping their parents on the land. None of this was at all popular with the peasantry or many urban artisans, particularly as familiar forms of welfare had collapsed with Church revenues. Hence there were local anti-French revolts throughout the 'three years' of French Republican rule, and they became particularly violent and widespread by 1798–9. An anti-revolutionary alliance was forged, of Crown, Church, and peasantry, desperate to preserve the old way of life and fiercely hostile to the French, to land enclosers, to the *patrioti* and Jacobins, and to the liberal intelligentsia with its 'enlightened' French ideas. Often, particularly in the south, the outcome was virtual local civil war, as rival factions – one 'Jacobin', the other 'legitimist' – literally battled for local or regional control. The most dramatic revolt was in the mainland south. Early in 1799 Cardinal Ruffo marched a vast disparate band of *Sanfedisti* peasant insurgents right up from Calabria to Naples, to fight the godless French. In Naples itself, up to 7,000 'enlightened' members of the middle and noble classes were massacred as 'Jacobins' by dockers and workers – a real slaughter of the intellectuals. But revolt was not restricted to the south. In Tuscany, too, the peasants rose, to the cry of *Viva Maria*! Moreover, resistance to the French could take other forms. Peasants often grazed their sheep on newly-enclosed land, in direct defiance of the new laws and the new municipal rulers; and they continued in their millions to observe the old religious practices like pilgrimages and local saints' days, banned by the new enlightened regime. It is not surprising, therefore, that when troops of the Russo-Austrian coalition retook Northern Italy in April 1799, they were generally welcomed. In Milan, the crowds cheered as the Austrians marched back in.

EMPIRE AND LAND

Later in 1799 the fortunes of war changed again, and Bonaparte returned. This time the French impact was longer, and deeper. The new puppet regimes lasted until 1814, although their frontiers were constantly redrawn, and their rulers constantly transferred. In 1805 the revived Cisalpine Republic – which after 1801 included Venetia west of the river Adige – became the Kingdom of Italy, with its capital in Milan and Napoleon Bonaparte as its absentee king. The north-west regions of Italy, including Piedmont, Liguria, Parma and the coastal parts of Tuscany and Latium, were simply annexed to France by 1805, and administered by French officials as *départements* of France. Other duchies and minor kingdoms were handed out to Napoleon's relatives or favourite generals. Tuscany was given to his sister Elisa; in 1811 his son became king of Rome; the Kingdom of Naples was run from 1806 by his brother Joseph, and after 1808 by his brother-in-law Joachim Murat. Even the regent in Milan, Eugène de Beauharnais, was Napoleon's stepson. By 1809, when the Papal States were also annexed to France, all mainland Italy was French-run, most of it in three forms: the north-west, ruled directly from Paris as part of the French Empire; the north-east, as the Kingdom of Italy (*Regno Italico*), governed by a regent in Milan; and the Kingdom of Naples under King Joachim. Once again, only the two southern islands escaped this new form of dynastic rule, providing havens instead for the former dynasties of Piedmont and Naples.

This time French rule was far more 'imperial' than 'republican'. Napoleon's regime had no time for Jacobin ideas, nor for the *patrioti* of the 1790s. The press was strictly censored; representative assemblies existed, but represented only the elite. Again, the various Napoleonic states needed educated middle-class support, from professional men and landowners, and normally received it. Even many of the nobility came round: by 1806 three-quarters of the Prefects in the Kingdom of Italy were aristocrats. There were plenty of jobs for the talented and qualified, in public administration, in teaching, in the greatly expanded police forces, and above all as officers in the army. By 1810 the Kingdom of Italy had 50,000 men under arms, and most of the officers were Italian.

Italians were now citizens of the 'Grand Empire'; they might serve in Paris, Germany, Spain, or Russia. They were torn away from their sleepy provincial backwaters and mobilised into a huge European enterprise, both civil and military – an enterprise portrayed, of course, not just as conquest or family aggrandizement, but as progress, as liberation of the peoples from the secular yokes of throne and altar. Thirty thousand Italians fought with the French in Spain, *against* a popular insurrection; 27,000 fought with Napoleon in Russia. Ideas of Italian 'independence' or unity, let alone of freedom and equality, faded away; but many Italians were trained in proper military academies, learned how justice and administration should be conducted impartially, and began to revere the modernizing, secular State.

Many others did not. Taxes remained very high, and food prices rose sharply during the wars. Italians were still forced to provide for French armies elsewhere, and indeed to fight in them. There may have been 50,000 men in the Kingdom of Italy's army, but a further 40,000 had fled, or deserted [41 *p. 27*]. Peasants fled to the hills to avoid conscription into Napoleon's army, or managed to desert; they became bandits, or smugglers, or joined a local armed resistance band, like that of the famous 'Fra Diavolo' in Calabria. Revolts remained common, particularly when Napoleon's Continental blockade after 1805 hampered much Italian trade. Major ports, like Genoa or Naples, became virtually derelict. In Calabria, bloody risings and land occupations continued for two years; there were revolts in Bologna in 1802, and in Vicenza in 1806. But the revolts were local, often a reaction to the arrival of conscription-sergeants or tax-gatherers. The French were not popular, but they were less unpopular than in the 1790s, partly because they came to terms with the Church, which had to accept state appointment of bishops but was allowed to resume some of her earlier functions. Unlike Spain or western Russia, Italy experienced no mass guerrilla rising with 'national' overtones in these years, except in the South Tyrol. 'Secret societies', however, became more numerous and significant, particularly in the south. They were of different kinds – some Jacobin, some Catholic, some 'moderate' and constitutional – but they all plotted for an uncertain future. The best known, the *Carbonari*,* came to southern Italy (from France itself) in 1806, originally as a 'moderate' society bent on securing and retaining ex-feudal and ecclesiastical lands.

The new French-dominated states, however unrevolutionary, continued many of the legal and economic policies of their predecessors in 1796–9. In particular, the surviving feudal jurisdictions, the very basis of state structure in some regions, were abolished (in 1806 in the Kingdom of Naples). So, too, were many other old 'corporate' privileges of particular areas or social groups – privileges enjoyed previously by guilds of artisans as well as by feudal aristocrats or churchmen. Henceforth all would be equal before the law, and the law would be administered by state officials, not feudal lords. As for inheritance, primogeniture was abolished, or severely curtailed. Thus the state would decide what a man might own, and to whom he might pass it on.

The key issue was land, and land tenure. Land was, after all, virtually the only source of wealth. The French overthrew centuries-old traditions, and replaced them by new-fangled ideas of small property and absolute ownership ('perfect property'), untrammelled by customary rights. The barons retained their private, non-feudal land, but the feudal estates themselves were sold off to new owners, as were the big ecclesiastical properties and much land owned by local councils (especially woodlands and grazing areas). It was a huge privatization of public assets, but outside Piedmont and a few mountain zones few peasants could afford to buy, or to pay the land taxes if they did. Those few who did formed a 'new class' of 'kulak' farm-owners, detested by their neighbours. Most of the purchasers were lesser nobles or urban lawyers and businessmen, anxious for the status and security that only landed property could provide. Some were top government officials and army officers, acquiring huge estates for themselves on the cheap: in Piedmont, the fathers and grandfathers of the heroes of the Risorgimento – Cavour, Balbo, d'Azeglio – served the French and established their own social, political and economic base. In the Kingdom of Naples, where much Church land was sold off, the nobles became greater landowners than they had been previously, although in 1815 there were also 200,000 new landowners compared with twenty years earlier [31 *p. 33*]. In Bologna province, where nobles had owned three-quarters of the private land in 1789, they still owned over half in 1815 [117 *pp. 95–7*].

In short, landownership was often still concentrated in the hands of the wealthy and powerful, just as in the *ancien régime*; but more of the professional and business classes had joined the wealthy and powerful. Moreover, the new legal codes gave landowners far more power to do as they wished with the land; and many common resources – whether formerly feudal, ecclesiastical, or municipal – were 'enclosed' by hedges and lost to the peasants. The social structure of most villages in the country was thus transformed. In hill and mountain areas the peasants usually acquired land, although it was often poor, unproductive land remote from markets. In most places the landlords' estates, and their power over their tenants, increased dramatically. The poor lost out, for ecclesiastical estates had financed what little welfare was available; new progressive 'workhouses' replaced old-fashioned charity. The loss of common lands was even more critical, for these had been the source of firewood for heating and cooking, and places where you could graze your sheep or pigs: they were vital to the rural dweller's subsistence.

THE RESULTS OF FRENCH RULE

It is, perhaps, easy to exaggerate the impact of these tumultuous years in Italy. In 1789 there had been thirteen Italian states, ruled either by absolutist monarchs (e.g. Piedmont and Naples), or by exclusive aristocratic castes (e.g. the republics of Venice and Genoa). Within a few years they had all been overthrown, and much of society had been transformed as well. However, the transformation was not as dramatic, at least in northern Italy, as has often been alleged. The divide between 'aristocrats' and 'bourgeois' had been less rigid in Italy than in some neighbouring countries: successful businessmen and lawyers could buy land and titles, while many eighteenth-century aristocrats improved their estates and engaged in trade. In Piedmont, the nobles owned only 10 per cent of the land in 1789, and the Church only 15 per cent. In Lombardy, the Austrian Emperor Joseph II had already abolished the barons' jurisdiction, closed down some of the monasteries, forbidden pilgrimages and insisted on civil marriages, long before the French revolutionary armies arrived. His brother Leopold had drawn up a new, 'enlightened' criminal code in Tuscany, which even abolished the death penalty. Even the changes in land tenure were less dramatic than might appear. Aristocratic landowners had usually been absentees, residing in cities; the feudal estates had actually been run by managers, mostly for their own benefit. What happened under the French was that the managers took over formal legal ownership as well. Even so, the French did provide a legal title for such men, and also a great deal of extra land, to benefit both them and the urban lawyers and merchants on whom French political power depended.

The real impact of the French was threefold. Firstly, legal and administrative decisions were now taken by state officials, who were always of the same type – urban, educated lawyers, expected to act according to fixed uniform rules and modern legal codes, and responsible to their superiors in a fixed hierarchy of command and promotion. These officials were not new in Italy, but they became far more numerous under the French, and they were successful. On the whole, the taxes were raised, the land was sold, and the conscripts were marched off. Many of the French-appointed officials kept their jobs for decades to come, long after the French had departed, and they continued to operate in the ways the French had taught them.

What they lacked, of course, was any accountability to the people. On the contrary, the French model created, or rather expanded, a state machinery with values quite distinct from the unplanned, superstitious, unenlightened peasant societies in which most Italians lived. Furthermore, the state was determined to remake that society in its own image.

The second major impact of French rule came, very simply, from war. For nearly twenty years Italy was wracked by war, constant, unpredictable and all-encroaching. The 'Italic army' of the Kingdom of Italy was the first institution for centuries that brought together key members of the (north) Italian elite in a common enterprise. Serving in such an army was an enormously important experience, particularly for the many officers who became enthusiastic converts to 'rational' progressive ideas. But even those who did not serve were affected by the war. Food prices rose steeply; trade and tourism were halted. No one was safe from marauding armies, nor from tax-gatherers and requisition officers.

The third result was in ideas, or 'mentalities'. Eighteenth-century Italy had, of course, been part of the European Enlightenment: devotees of 'rational' decision-making, believers in rights and legal procedures, advocates of progress and general education, had been common enough. But the French revolutionary armies brought a harsher, tougher version to Italy. The 'Rights of Man' meant, at least initially, war on ancient laws and ancient privileges; they meant, too, freedom for property-owners to do as they wished with their own, heedless of communal practices like common grazing. They also meant a serious attack on the Church and her influence. Monks and friars were expelled from their ancient convents; Church estates were sequestered and sold off to the wealthy; Church festivals, pilgrimages and processions were banned. As for the poor, traditional alms-giving and begging were no longer tolerated; 'from welfare to work' was the answer, in the form of workhouses where the poor would learn to be useful citizens. Schooling, too, became secular and compulsory, and taught values that were not religious but sober and patriotic – the stern voice of duty, of service to the People and to the State. In short, the French brought in a real *Kulturkampf*, a clash of incompatible values. And this was not a tolerant age; both sides fought for their beliefs.

Few Italians accepted the revolutionary package of the 1790s in its entirety, but nearly all lived under authoritarian secular regimes after 1800, and were exposed to the new ideas. By 1812, however, Napoleon was in retreat from Moscow, and French power was manifestly declining. Who could tell what would follow? In non-occupied Sicily, the king granted a constitution on British lines, and with British prompting. It promised freedom of speech, of the press and so on, the end of feudalism, and a two-chamber legislature, of Lords and elected Commons. Such a constitution, or the similar Spanish one of the same year, became the demand of 'moderate' property-owners throughout Italy: they believed it would guarantee order, and an elite input into decision-making in the post-Napoleonic era. Other Italians hoped for a more dramatic outcome. Secret societies, with their elaborate oaths and rituals and their promise of conspiracy and plotting, had become endemic during the years of French rule, and in 1814 they thought their hour had come.

This was the real legacy of the French regimes. The old stable Italy had been destroyed. Men hoped, or feared, that society could easily be restructured by its rulers. But who, now, had a legitimate claim to rule? Italians found themselves living in a conflict-ridden, uncertain world where people could no longer trust their neighbours, and where plots and violent insurrections were commonplace. Such a world required strong government, but by 1814 the French were in retreat.

3 THE RESTORATION STATES

As French power collapsed in 1814, the 'moderates' who had enjoyed some status and local power under French rule had reason to feel fearful. Aspirations to Italian independence and/or unity were not totally forgotten, and indeed in Naples King Joachim abandoned Napoleon and proclaimed an independent Italian state, but he found few supporters. The 'moderates' hoped, above all, to avoid a simple return to royal absolutism. They therefore advocated constitutional government, with elected legislatures, and knew that the victorious British would support them. But Austria, not Britain, was the dominant Coalition Power on the Continent, and after 1814 she directly governed much of northern Italy. The Austrian Emperor had no wish to rule constitutionally, and saw no reason to rely on Italian middle-class lawyers. A constitution therefore remained an aspiration, not a reality; but it was an important aspiration, and it did remain.

The political framework of post-Napoleonic Italy was decided at the Congress of Vienna in 1814–15, largely to suit the Austrians. Italy remained, as she had been since the sixteenth century, a plaything of the European Powers, although at least those powers now sought peace and stability rather than war. The pre-1796 situation was not restored. Italy was divided into five reasonably large states: Piedmont (generally known as the 'Kingdom of Sardinia', and including that island as well as Nice and Savoy north of the Alps); Lombardy-Venetia; the Grand Duchy of Tuscany; the Papal States; and the Kingdom of Naples (including Sicily, and formally known after 1816 as the 'Kingdom of the Two Sicilies'). The treaty also established, or ratified, several smaller duchies in Emilia and northern Tuscany: Lucca, under a 'Spanish' Bourbon, which was merged into Tuscany in 1847; Massa and Carrara, retained by its duchess until she died in 1829, when it was absorbed by Modena; Parma and Piacenza, whose duchess was Maria Luisa, daughter of a Habsburg emperor and second wife of Napoleon (her lover and future second husband, an Austrian count, actually ran the place); and Modena, under the half-Austrian Francis IV of Austria-Este, an able man who detested the Habsburgs and was married to a daughter of the King of Piedmont. San Marino remained an independent republic.

Austria gained the most. She recovered her eighteenth- century possession of Lombardy and acquired the former Venetian Republic, which both now became parts of the Habsburg Empire. She also dominated Tuscany, where the Grand Duke was brother of the Austrian Emperor, and the Central Italian duchies. Furthermore, she had great influence over the Papal States, and kept garrisons at Ferrara and Comacchio within them; the Austrians could, and sometimes did, move troops into the rest of Papal-run Emilia-Romagna, to crush rebellion and restore order. In northern Italy, the Austrians' only rival was Piedmont, which acquired Liguria – the old Republic of Genoa – as part of the Vienna settlement. In the south, the Bourbon King Ferdinand IV of Naples and III of Sicily resumed sway over his two very different and mutually hostile kingdoms. In 1816 he abolished the Sicilian constitution granted four years earlier and unified his realms, becoming Ferdinand I of the Two Sicilies. He too was allied to Austria. It is worth noting that all these dynastic rulers had family origins – usually fairly recent family origins – outside Italy, and several still ruled territory elsewhere. Arguably the only truly 'Italian' ruler was the Pope, but he of course was an international figure, leader of a worldwide Church, rather than merely the ruler of the Papal States.

The Italian States were, in fact, part of a complex European system. Italy after 1815 reflected the interests of the victorious European Powers, anxious to prevent a French revival and to keep the French out of Northern Italy in future. That was why Piedmont was given Liguria, to create a greater bulwark against France; that was why Austria was given Venetia, and allowed to dominate the rest of north-central Italy. The new regimes, however precarious they may have seemed at home, were backed by the other European Powers. Even France did not mind too much. Italy was weak and divided, and in the long run that suited French interests too.

THE ITALIAN REGIMES

Not that the new regimes were particularly precarious at home, at least initially. In Venice, in October 1813, the local people had warmly welcomed the Austrians as liberators from the tyrannical French. In Tuscany the Grand Dukes ruled with a light rein, allowed the nobility status and local power, and were reasonably popular except in the fractious port of Livorno. The press was fairly free, and even the 'secret societies' were allowed to operate quite openly. In Lombardy most of the older nobles, as well as the artisans, clergy, and commercial classes, probably favoured the Habsburg restoration as a guarantee of peace and stability. However, the younger nobles and many professional people, government officials and intellectuals had absorbed French ideas over the previous twenty years, and expected – at the very least – a 'constitutional' regime with a high degree of autonomy from Vienna. But it was not to be. Lombardy under the Austrians had no constitution, and no autonomy. The intellectuals, and the penurious local nobles, soon began to grumble. Even so, the most discontented noble elites in Italy in 1816 were the Sicilians, who detested the Neapolitans and were deprived of the 1812 constitution which had given them considerable power; and the Genoese, who had also hoped for constitutional government (under British protection) and who disliked Piedmontese rule almost as much as did the Sardinians, who had been subject to it since 1720. It was no coincidence that Genoa soon became a major focus of 'republican and radical insurrection (Giuseppe Mazzini himself was Genoese); or that Sicily remained in more or less constant revolt for most of the nineteenth century, revolt often encouraged or fomented by the upper classes.

Elsewhere, however, the restored regimes were accepted not too unwillingly. The great question in all cases was: how much to restore? In Piedmont, until 1821, the answer was easy: everything. Victor Emanuel I came back to Turin from his Sardinian exile in May 1814, determined to rule as if the French invasions had never been. The day after his arrival he decreed that all laws passed under the French were abolished; all those appointed to official jobs by the French were dismissed. The old aristocrats were restored to power and privilege in army and civil affairs. The Church, in particular the Jesuits, recovered their dominance of education, although little of their land. Piedmont became, yet again, 'half barracks, half cloister'. However, the French way of controlling local government was retained, as were most of the new French taxes and the new French police. Moreover, some of the French-appointed army officers were simply indispensable, and had to be brought back very hastily in 1815 during the 'Hundred Days'.

The restored system was not a success. The large number of ex-Napoleonic officers, now dismissed or downgraded, soon became a serious threat to the regime. In 1821, after an attempted military coup by officers with modernising, 'French' ideas, Victor Emanuel was forced to abdicate. His successors Charles Felix (1821–31) and, especially, Charles Albert (1831–49) had learned the lesson. Although just as autocratic, militarist and anti-liberal, they at least saw the need to modernize administration, justice, and communications. Charles Felix, in fact, disliked Turin and spent much of his time travelling round his dominions; so he built decent roads and ports. Moreover, he was willing to give top jobs not only to Piedmontese aristocrats but also to middle-class Sardinians, whom he had learned to trust during his long years as viceroy on the island. Charles Albert brought in new civil, criminal and commercial codes of law, set up a council of state on the French model, and abolished feudalism in Sardinia. However, the press was still strictly censored (even words like 'Italy' and 'nation' were taboo) and there was no freedom of association, nor representation. Charles Albert relied on his aristocracy, and knew how to appreciate blue blood. He flattered the nobles, received them graciously at Court, and bestowed decorations and fancy titles with a generous spirit. In Piedmont, unlike the rest of northern Italy, the local nobles held the top jobs and helped run the state machinery. Even so, being an aristocrat was not sufficient in itself – the king insisted on competence and educational qualifications too. A 'modernizing alliance' between crown and nobility gradually took shape, of great importance for the future. This did not apply in Liguria, where the old patricians stayed in Genoa, cut off from office and nursing their grievances; but in Piedmont itself the educated elite basked content in the warm glow of royal favour.

In Lombardy things were rather different. The Austrians installed a viceroy in Milan, for ceremonial and court purposes, but the viceroy's court was dreary and noticeably reluctant to recognize Italian noble titles – the Austrians even set up a special commission to investigate the nobles' lineage, and its scrutiny was often embarrassingly thorough [109 *p. 62*]. Nor were the nobles' vast military or administrative abilities often recognized either, even at local level. The Austrian administration was headed by an Austrian governor, tightly supervised from Vienna, and the top jobs in the civil service and judiciary were reserved for Austrians. In return, the local aristocrats refused to admit the Austrians to their elegant *salons*, or to serve in the Austrian army. Moreover, the middle classes suffered discrimination too. Lawyers operated according to the Austrian legal code, and so had to know German; hence the bilingual South Tyrolese took the best cases. Universities and schools followed a curriculum laid down in Vienna. For the Lombards, Austrian rule came to mean rule by snobbish German-speaking foreigners; competent, it was true, but uninspiring and unfriendly. Since many north Italian landowners had property in both Lombardy and Piedmont, they could in effect choose their allegiance;

and they chose Piedmont. Even Count Casati, the Austrian-appointed mayor of Milan, sent his sons to the Turin military academy, so they became officers in the Piedmontese army that was, by the 1840s, preparing to fight against Austria.

In Venetia the Austrians were less unpopular. Their rule was generally seen as better than that of the French, and they were more reassuringly clerical than the French had been, or than the Piedmontese would be. There were few 'subversives', and those few wanted a restored Venetian Republic rather than anything larger. Still, even in Venetia the disaffected middle classes – lawyers and doctors who could not find jobs – became more numerous as time went on. Top posts in the Venetian administration were held by Austrians, or Czechs, or even by Lombards, but rarely by Venetians.

In the south, the Kingdom of the Two Sicilies arguably had two 'Restorations': in 1815–16, and again in the early 1820s after the failure of the 1820–1 revolt (see pp. 36–7). Both involved severe police repression and a purge of the army and of the French-influenced *Murattiani** in the police, judiciary, civil service and schools. However, both periods were short, and both soon degenerated into disputes between rival factions and families. Even after 1821 many *Carbonari*, compromised during the revolt, seem to have kept their jobs. After 1821, in fact, the mainland south was fairly stable. 'French' institutions – a centralized administration, Napoleonic codes of law and so forth – remained in being, taxes were low and protective tariffs were high. In the provinces, Bourbon officials were allowed to reside in their own home town, and so were usually chosen from the local nobles or 'notables'; in practice, government jobs were quasi-hereditary, and centralization was a myth. In Naples itself, 'populist' (*lazzaronesco*) absolutism, run by aristocrats and lawyers but careful to provide bread and circuses, worked remarkably well, whatever the intellectuals thought of it.

Sicily was a different matter. The Bourbons could not control the island and had no allies, except inasmuch as Catania and Messina could usually be relied on to oppose any 'autonomous' move suggested by Palermo. The Sicilian nobles, nostalgic for the 'British' constitution granted them in 1812 and suppressed in 1816, had no intention of giving up any privileges or traditions, and were even more of a problem to royal officials than was the riotous peasantry. 'Sicilianism' was conservative and aristocratic, but it was a real separatist threat to the weak and remote Bourbon government in Naples. By the late 1830s some of the middle-class 'democrats' were becoming separatist too.

As for the Papal States, there too there were fitful, but never implemented, efforts at central control. These states were confusingly diverse – each region was run by a 'Cardinal-Legate', but had its own laws and administration. In Emilia-Romagna and the Marches lay courts and much of the Napoleonic civil code, apart from divorce, survived after 1815; further south canon law and church courts were the norm. 'Clerical government' was a grievance, particularly among the nobles of Emilia-Romagna who would otherwise have controlled those areas [*Doc. 1*]. The Papal States were, indeed, run by cardinals and prelates, although it is worth remembering that often these officials were in fact Roman noblemen, clerical only in title and dress. Even Cardinal Consalvi, who virtually ruled Rome until 1823 as Pius VII's greatly respected Secretary of State, never became a priest. After 1823, however, the *zelanti** were more influential and clerical control became tighter. In 1831 the ambassadors of the European Powers urged Pope Gregory XVI to set up a 'lay' civil service and judiciary, and to permit some local councils to be elected. This he rejected, but some appointed councils were revived in the 'Legations'* of Emilia-Romagna. For most of the Restoration period Rome itself was tranquil and relatively prosperous, but the nobles and gentry of Emilia-Romagna, after twenty years of secular French rule, were far less happy with their lot.

THE FRENCH LEGACY: ADMINISTRATION AND THE ARMY

Most states after 1815, including Lombardy-Venetia, Tuscany and the Two Sicilies, retained many of the French innovations and some of the French aspirations. Their rulers liked having a centralized, obedient administrative machine. They approved, too, of a single uniform code of laws, applicable to all, and of French tax-gathering techniques – however rapacious, they certainly brought the money in. Abolition of the ancient privileges, enjoyed previously by nobles, clergy or city corporation, had naturally enhanced royal power, and so was quietly continued. The Church, in particular, regained her former privileges and immunities only in the Papal States and, to a lesser degree, in Piedmont (in both cases they became a focus of liberal anti-clericalism). Restoration governments, however ramshackle or inefficient they may have been, were less so than their predecessors before 1796; they were also less arbitrary and more 'rule-bound', perhaps even more 'rational'.

One French innovation was particularly important. The paramilitary police force, the *gendarmerie*, had proved extremely useful in combatting rural banditry. Even Piedmont decided to keep it in 1814, suitably renamed as the *carabinieri*. In the towns, too, policing – especially secret policing – was one of the great legacies of the French era, enthusiastically adopted by all successor States. The Chief of Police became, arguably, the most important public official. Restoration governments feared French ideas and feared revolution; so they adopted the key institution of the French Revolution.

Even so, policing was not particularly repressive, before 1848, nor was it particularly successful. The urban police were few and ill-trained. They could infiltrate the secret societies and revolutionary cells easily enough, but they did not dare to touch the really dangerous people, e.g. the popular leaders (*capipopolo**) among the urban artisans, let alone the liberal students or enlightened nobles. Indeed, the later 'liberal' propaganda that Restoration governments were viciously harsh and repressive is simply not tenable. Only two people were executed in Piedmont after the army insurrection of 1821; two, again, in Naples after the 1820–1 rising. Even censorship was mild, particularly in Tuscany and Lombardy, partly because it was now done by the police rather than the Church. The problem was not that the regimes were repressive, but that they were not repressive enough. They often failed to maintain law and order, especially in the rural areas of Venetia, the Legations and the south, where 'civic militias' of loyal peasants proved to be neither loyal nor disciplined. Italy remained an armed and dangerous country, where men settled their disputes by arms. Governments could respect property rights but they could not guarantee personal security, and became a great deal less 'legitimate' as a result [38, 64, 97].

The key institution of the Restoration States, as of the French Empire, was the army. But the officer corps' loyalty was suspect, particularly in the early years. Many of the most experienced officers and NCOs had served in the 'Italic army' under Napoleon, and were steeped in its ways and ideas. After 1815 these men were often purged, and in any case states had less need for large armies. But dismissals still left the problem of disaffected ex-officers looking for work, and there were still plenty of disaffected officers left in service. Army revolts – palace coups by senior officers and nobles – were successful, for a time, in Naples in 1820–1 and Piedmont in 1821 (and 1833) (see pp. 36–7). The officers' demand in these cases was for a constitution, i.e. for liberties; in both cases the Austrians had to intervene, to restore order and kingly rule. In short, the Italian Restoration States could not rely on the loyalty even of their own senior officers, and were easy to overthrow. Even Piedmont, the most 'independent' state in Italy, relied ultimately on Austrian force. The dukedoms of central Italy, including Tuscany, had no real armies at all, and were even more reliant on Vienna. So was the Pope, although he had over 10,000 men under arms in 1820, largely for policing purposes. But the Austrians were overstretched. They had to control not only Italy but a huge unruly empire in Central Europe, and they could keep only a relatively small standing army in Italy. Meanwhile what were poor noblemen, with surplus sons, to do? The sons would no longer go into the Church, nor could they easily join the local army. In Rome Cardinal Consalvi recognized the problem. He founded a new 'Noble Guard' specifically to satisfy the aristocrats' needs, but it only had 120 members, and they received no pay.

The Restoration States also had serious problems with their administrative machinery. They nearly all retained the French structure and purged only the top personnel, and even so many senior administrators had to be brought back later. In Piedmont Prospero Balbo, who had served the French faithfully for years and had been dismissed in 1814, was Minister of the Interior by 1819. Most of the younger officials remained in post: thousands of French-appointed officials, young or youngish in 1815, filled most of the available jobs for decades to come. Like the army officers, they remained under a cloud of suspicion, and were treated with marked parsimony. Young 'officials' or judges in Lombardy-Venetia or Piedmont often held lowly, unpaid jobs for years – twelve years was normal in Lombardy in the 1830s – in the hope of eventual appointment to a paid post. Most administrators were middle-class law graduates, supported by their families early on, and none too loyal to their governments. The system was, indeed, calculated to encourage disloyalty, corruption and celibacy. The top jobs, of course, were reserved for aristocrats, or in Lombardy-Venetia for 'foreigners'. Centralized administration was a pyramid, with a seething mass of resentful officials at its base, and even more would-be officials outside. It may have seemed satisfactory to the rulers, but not to the administrators themselves, nor to the ruled.

To summarize, most Restoration governments were neither particularly 'reactionary' nor repressive. They adopted, and adapted, 'French' administrative and legal innovations – codes of law, impartial justice, efficient policing, sometimes even educational systems. Apart from the Papal States, they were 'secular', and by the 1830s they were bent on modernization and improvements, particularly of roads, railways and ports. There was even some attempt at representation, or at least consultation. Non-elected consultative councils, called 'congregations', existed in Lombardy-Venetia, Tuscany and Parma at local, provincial and central level; Piedmont (from 1831), Naples and Sicily each had state councils to advise the monarch. It is true that these bodies were full of nobles and landowners, who represented nobody but themselves, and that they had virtually no authority anyway, but they showed that some effort was thought desirable to integrate the social and economic elite into the political system. This was more marked at local government level. Smaller municipalities in Lombardy-Venetia had genuine elected local councils, although even there mayors were appointed from above. Elsewhere local councillors were appointed too, usually from the local landowners. This was not, perhaps, as centralist or autocratic as might appear. At least local government was given clearly defined powers. Moreover, memories of the massacres of revolutionary times were still strong. For decades to come fierce family vendettas continued at local level, centred on whose side your father or grandfather had been on in 1799, 1814, or 1821, and exacerbated by squabbles over land purchases. In these circumstances the government intendant's appointment of local authorities was the lesser evil: elected local councils would have been disastrous.

Despite the plots and insurrections against them, the various states were not likely to collapse, as long as Austria remained strong. Yet they did have a legitimacy problem, or several problems. Except for Piedmont and perhaps Tuscany, they did not manage to win enough support, particularly elite and aristocratic support. They often spent much time and effort trying to protect the citizens' civil, legal and property rights, but they could not formally proclaim they were doing so, in written constitutions. Nor could they grant political rights, to representation, assembly, or suffrage; and there was no fully free press or right of free speech, however tolerant some of the regimes were in practice. These were strongly-felt grievances among the educated. It is noticeable how until the 1830s revolts always focused on demands for a constitution, rarely on a call for unification. Then there was regional disaffection. The Italian states may have been small, but not so small as to avoid being rent by regional rivalries. Even the more stable and successful states had rebellious outlying provinces, where it was difficult for the state to enforce its rule: Liguria, Livorno, Sicily, Emilia-Romagna. Finally, there were lots of dissatisfied non-noble (and some noble) job-seekers with a grievance, mostly professional men desperate for political change. A lawyer without political friends and connections would win few cases, and would have few clients. Some of the later 'heroes of the Risorgimento', like Francesco Crispi, turned to revolutionary politics only after failing, several times, to gain a state job.

In short, governments were nothing like as bad as the 'liberal' or 'national' propagandists claimed, but they did fail to win the support of key people. There may have been few revolutionaries and no real revolutionary threat most of the time, but there was disaffection, particularly dangerous among the elite and the palace guard. At least two Restoration rulers – Charles Albert in Piedmont and Duke Francis IV of Modena – were themselves briefly involved in plots, or counter-plots. In bad years food riots were always possible too, by urban artisans or peasants. Restoration governments were nervous governments, and had reason to be.

4 RESTORATION: SOCIETY AND ECONOMY

THE POLITICS OF LAND

Throughout the Restoration period, indeed throughout the nineteenth century, the real political issue was not constitutional liberty, nor independence, nor unification, but land. The great land redistribution under the French led to constant political and legal disputes, particularly in the south. Who, after all, could prove a legal title to land held by custom for centuries? Countless legal cases dragged on interminably. Some landowners found themselves dispossessed, and fought back angrily against the usurpers. It became vital to have a good lawyer, with some political connections, and kinship or patronage networks were also reinforced. It was also vital to control local government, which was selling off the best ex-feudal or municipal land, or to be on good terms with those who did. Local politics thus became the focus of fierce faction disputes and endemic hatreds among the leading families. But in the last resort land, even if acquired legally, could only be protected from angry neighbours by force. Armed squads sprang up, to defend their own land and usurp that of their rivals. Public order, always fragile, broke down in the struggle for land. Poor peasants were, needless to say, squeezed off any land they might possess, and lost their access to formerly common land as well. In short, the French privatization programme triggered endemic rural conflict, particularly in southern Italy, throughout the early nineteenth century. The one common feature of this rural disorder was that rioting peasants demanded 'their' land back, or occupied it by force.

Restoration governments were faced, therefore, with an intractable set of problems. Restoring the pre-French status quo was not an option; it would have caused even more trouble than they had already. But much ecclesiastical or ex-feudal land had not yet been sold off; what should be done with it? What counted as a legal title to land? Which rights did landownership include? What about traditional 'use-rights' (*usi civici*), such as rights of way, rights to pasture and fishing, to gather wood and the like, which non-owners had always enjoyed and which were often vital to their subsistence? How could forests and water resources be preserved, in the new age of private property? How could food production be increased, and the land become more profitable?

In most states there was no acceptable answer to most of these questions – acceptable, that is, to the various local factions. Only in Piedmont, perhaps, was there relative economic (and hence political) stability, for most small peasants there had acquired farms on ex-Church or ex-feudal land. In 1852 there were almost 800,000 landed properties in Piedmont, which had a population of 3.75 million. Elsewhere the picture was more confused. In much of the south the aristocrats, who often controlled local government, did well out of the sale of Church land and ended up owning even more land than previously. In some areas, particularly in lower Lombardy and Venetia, commercially-minded tenant farmers took over the land, legally or *de facto*; sometimes it was the more ambitious or cunning peasants who won out. But one factor was virtually constant. Everywhere common land was under attack. It was usurped by the powerful; it was sold off by local councillors (to themselves or their relatives); it was sold off by government decree, as in Venetia after 1839; it was enclosed against sheep. Indeed, enclosure of the commons was one episode in the secular Mediterranean war of 'settled' farmers and peasants against 'nomadic' shepherds and cattle grazers, who had used common land for pasture. Most important of all, privatizing the commons meant cutting down trees, particularly by the 1840s when railway-building led to a huge demand for sleepers. Deforestation had all the predictable environmental consequences: reduced rainfall, soil erosion, flash floods taking away topsoil, and stagnant water in the valleys causing more malaria.

It has often been said that the Napoleonic land reforms dispossessed the old landowning aristocracy and put land into the hands of more commercially-minded, 'bourgeois' owners from the towns. This did occur occasionally, particularly among the tenant farmers of the Lombard plains, but it was far from universal. The old aristocrats may have lost their feudal privileges but they retained a surprising amount of land – particularly the best agricultural land on plains, and highly profitable building land near cities. It was not their land that was sold off in the early nineteenth century, but that of the Church, Crown and municipality, and nobles often managed to buy it. Aristocrats owned about 30 per cent of the cultivated land in Lombardy in the 1830s, over half in the Bolognese region, at least a quarter in Umbria [84 *pp. 165–6*]. And 'bourgeois' landowners were rarely ruthless commercial exploiters. Just as often they were lawyers or retired civil servants, seeking a rural retreat and a bit of social status.

In any case, 'aristocrats' and 'bourgeoisie' were not that distinct in Italy. Noble landowners were just as likely to 'improve' their land as bourgeois ones; both were anxious to enjoy the benefits of a larger market. Most noblemen lived in the cities, and indeed outnumbered the commercial middle classes there: Milan in 1838 had 3,000 resident noblemen, compared with less than 1,000 merchants, bankers and manufacturers, and 170 advocates and notaries [115 *p. 286*]. Nobles followed a profession, often engaged in trade and sometimes even married into rich 'bourgeois' families – some heroes of the Risorgimento were born of such unions. Both groups now wore the same clothes, joined the same prestigious agrarian associations or improvement societies, went to the same clubs and theatres, and read the same newspapers. Sometimes they even attended the same universities. By mid-century they were not so much allying as fusing into a single elite. This did not happen everywhere, of course: the Roman and (less markedly) the Sicilian aristocracies remained as aloof as ever, and there was plenty of snobbishness in Piedmont. Nonetheless, the recognition of common interests and values by the old landed aristocrats and the newly-landed middle classes was hugely important. Some historians see it as the key to understanding the Risorgimento [46 *p. 305*]. It created an effective new elite, used to acting together and less beholden to the existing states.

One real problem for many landowners was the French inheritance law. At least half the property, sometimes more, had to be equally divided among their offspring, including girls. In time, this would lead to serious fragmentation of landholdings, and that is exactly what happened in the hill zones of Piedmont, and in Sardinia. Various strategies existed to avoid this outcome. A landowner might have fewer children, by marrying late; this strategy was much practised by peasant owners. Or he might marry cousins, thus ensuring that the land would stay in the family; this was quite common in the south. Or he might discourage all his children, except the eldest son, from marrying at all, so that his grandchildren would eventually inherit substantial property when their unmarried uncles and aunts died off. This last strategy was common among the richer and noble landowners. However, it was risky: the family might die out altogether, if the eldest son had no surviving offspring. Another big snag was that it meant most members of the elite did not marry. They continued to live at home in 'patriarchal' households, squabbling with each other and still, as adults, subject to parental control.

In other respects landowners enjoyed fairly favourable times. True, grain prices slumped after the Napoleonic wars, but they rose slowly from the mid-1820s. Throughout Italy cereal productivity rose too, perhaps by 25 per cent from the mid-1820s to the late 1850s [107 *p.* 43]. Corn Laws, though lifted in bad years, protected home farmers from too much overseas competition. As common land came under the plough, and as marshes were drained by dukes and popes, the agricultural area itself increased, perhaps by as much as 10 per cent. Moreover, the population was increasing sharply, from an estimated 17.8 million in 1800 to 24 million in 1850, so demand for food went up and agricultural wages fell. The general picture is of a fairly rapid increase in food production, but an even more rapid increase in population. This meant that living standards declined, food shortages were always probable, and local famines were fairly common. Outside Lombardy and some wine-producing areas of Tuscany and Sicily, few farmers exported much of their products. Millions of small peasant-owners aimed at self-sufficiency, as did Tuscan sharecroppers and even the Southern *latifondo* estates, except in outstanding years. In bad years – 1815–17, 1830–32, and above all the mid-1840s – Italy relied heavily on grain imports. Bread was subsidized, and the poor were given public works jobs. In the 1840s so many people needed this support that government finances became strained throughout the peninsula, but at least a general famine was averted. Early in 1847 food prices had doubled in two years, but a good harvest in that year soon brought them down again.

SOCIAL CHANGE

As the population rose, so some cities grew rapidly. Turin had 75,000 inhabitants in 1800, 170,000 by 1860; Milan had 139,000 in 1814, 189,000 in 1847, and 240,000 in 1861 [115 *pp.* 283–4]. Venice, on the other hand, grew relatively slowly in the early nineteenth century, as did Palermo; and even Naples only rose from 350,000 in 1800 to 449,000 fifty years later. Even so, Naples remained by far the largest city in Italy, and one of the largest in Europe. The cities, with their charities and welfare relief, were a magnet for the nearby rural poor. In Rome, it was claimed that one-sixth of the inhabitants were vagrants or immigrants, living hand to mouth on handouts, begging, petty crime and casual jobs. Most of the jobs available to immigrants were in building or in domestic service: there were 20,000 servants in Turin alone. But there were never enough jobs for everybody. Even in smaller towns like Lodi a quarter of the population were paupers receiving assistance in 1830; the town council was trying desperately to stem the flow of rural incomers [38 *p. 70*]. Mass immigration meant a crisis in housing, hygiene, water supply and welfare. In Milan, the number of new-born babies abandoned by their mothers rose from about 800 p.a. in the late eighteenth century to well over 4000 in the 1850s, i.e. to more than a third of all babies born in the city (although admittedly some mothers received their own child back the next day, after they had registered as wet-nurses in order to be paid by the municipality).

The huge numbers of poor led to drastic remedies. In 1814–15 it had been generally accepted that charitable relief should largely be restored to the Church. But the Church tended to spend the money on ancient purposes no longer fashionable, like masses for the dead. Catholics also approved of almsgiving and thus, in 'liberal' eyes, encouraged begging. By the 1830s municipal or state-run welfare seemed more appropriate to reformers. Welfare recipients should be housed in institutions – orphanages, poorhouses, hospitals, asylums, prisons – where they would be a good deal less visible. To allow thousands of 'beggars on the streets' was a shameful reproach to enlightened modern government. Beggars were also thought (wrongly) to be a threat to property and to public order. Poorhouses became common. In 1836 Piedmont opened workhouses, and tried to force all the 'undeserving poor' (able-bodied beggars) into them. But how to distinguish between them and the 'deserving' or 'shamefaced' poor, honest toilers who had fallen into poverty through no fault of their own?

As for public health, despite the food shortages it could have been a lot worse. The plague had disappeared, and there were no more wars after 1814. Cholera, however, remained a real threat: 27,000 people died in Palermo in 1837, and there were also major outbreaks in Genoa and Naples. In one respect the poor in northern Italy were well off compared to their counterparts elsewhere in Europe. In Lombardy-Venetia free medical care was available, provided by qualified doctors or surgeons paid by the local municipality. Lombardy alone had 846 such doctors in 1857 (and 1,278 midwives), about half the total number of doctors in the region [45 *p. 158*] [*Doc. 2*]. Indeed, newly-qualified doctors had little option but to take municipal posts, working out three-year contracts in remote villages. To the rural poor they brought vaccination, hygienic advice and high-minded precepts, particularly about the evils of excessive drink. They must have helped 'modernize' the outlook of innumerable peasants. Even so, the northern peasants' diet changed for the worse in these years. Maize tended to replace wheat, and this exposed people to the vitamin-deficiency disease pellagra, an increasing scourge by mid-century, as was malaria in central and southern Italy.

Most Italians were, of course, illiterate; this was particularly the case among peasants, southerners, and women. On the other hand, from the 1830s many primary schools were founded in the towns and even in some northern rural areas. In Austrian-run Lombardy-Venetia primary schooling was compulsory for both sexes; it was nearly always provided by the local priests, who were expected to act as schoolmasters. The result was that most urban artisans in northern Italy, and many peasants, could read and write by 1850. It was embarrassing, for patriotic liberal reformers, that the Austrians ran a better school system than anyone else in Italy, particularly as the teachers were mostly priests; so they concentrated instead on the need for nursery education and technical secondary schools. These latter were also fairly common in the towns of Lombardy-Venetia by the 1840s, as were 'self-help' evening classes for adults in technical and scientific subjects.

Post-Restoration Italy was still a deeply Catholic country. Education and poor relief remained mostly in Church hands, as did hospitals. Doctors were mostly Catholic, unlike their successors later in the century, and worked closely with local priests. Before 1848 no-one supposed religion was incompatible with 'national' sentiment. Many Catholic intellectuals favoured a 'lay' state, but one in which the Church would retain a large social and cultural role. Yet the Church's position was not so secure as it appeared. Much of her land had been sold off, and her revenues thereby greatly reduced. Priests no longer received tithes, and now had to pay taxes. Church courts, abolished by the French, were not restored except in Piedmont and Modena. Many monasteries and convents, closed down by the French, stayed closed, even in the Papal States. Tuscany lost almost two-thirds of its monks and nuns; the diocese of Turin, which had had 93 male monasteries in 1780, had 30 in 1837; only 400 monasteries and convents in the Kingdom of Naples had been restored by 1821, out of the 1300 suppressed by the French. All this was not necessarily bad for the Church, for many ex-monks became parish priests instead, but it did often deprive rural areas not only of their religious centres but also of their sources of welfare and learning. In the south, the Church was now so poor that 50 dioceses were suppressed by 1834 [28 *p. 107*]. In the north, traditional charitable practices were being challenged by new hard-headed doctrines. In central Italy, papal rule in Emilia-Romagna was deeply unpopular with the people who mattered; and the three Popes from 1823 to 1846 were generally regarded as obscurantist reactionaries, much given to denouncing liberalism and religious tolerance. The Church felt threatened by the modern world. She therefore signed concordats with the various states to safeguard her role, but that simply tied her more closely to the existing regimes. In the Kingdom of Naples, clergy were expected not only to run the schools but to report to the authorities on the morals and opinions of state officials.

Land was not quite the only respectable source of wealth or income, but the professions did not flourish in early nineteenth-century Italy. There were too many lawyers and doctors for the available clients, and every year the universities produced more. At Padua, the number of law students quadrupled between 1817 and 1842 [41 p. 220]. They became 'quasi-professionals' – tutors, part-time teachers or journalists, seeking a niche in an overcrowded world. Jobs in state administration, teaching or the law were rare and ill-paid (see p. 23). This was very significant. Inasmuch as there is a plausible 'economic' or 'social' explanation for the Risorgimento, it lies here. The really 'dangerous classes' were not the urban poor, nor even the riotous artisans, but the unemployed professionals whose only hope of advancement lay in radical political change. They were 'bourgeois' all right, but not commercial, let alone industrial: they sought posts in the bureaucracy, and they usually sought in vain.

TRADE AND INDUSTRY

In commerce and industry the money also came from government 'jobs', not from market trading. It was governments which ordered ships and built ports, whose armies had to be clothed and fed, and whose criminals needed to be immured. An 'entrepreneur' was a man who was granted – or who bought from the Crown – these monopolies. This was particularly true of salt and tobacco merchants: these goods were state monopolies, manufactured and sold by 'contractors' at high prices, to benefit themselves and the Crown. In Naples, contractors controlled the grain supply, bringing it round from Apulia in their own ships. These 'merchants' may have been traders and 'bourgeois', but they had no interest in free trade, nor in liberal ideas, nor in 'national unity'. On the contrary, their entire income depended on monopolies, and on favours from the existing states. Often they had lent large sums to the governments as well. And even when merchants were genuine international traders, as at Livorno or Ancona, they still had little interest in national unification, which would have removed the privileged 'free-port' status of their home towns. Indeed, perhaps the real economic weakness of post-1815 Italy was in its commerce. There were simply too many restraints on trade: guilds, privileges, monopolies, high excise duties even on food, above all a host of frontiers and customs posts; until 1822 there were even customs barriers between Lombardy and Venetia. People could not trade easily within Italy, let alone elsewhere. The Milanese, for example, were discouraged from using Genoa, a big handicap in reaching many markets, and much resented [37, 104].

As for industry, it was carried on by thousands of self-employed craftsmen in every town – tailors, joiners, cobblers, jewellers and the like – often providing luxury goods to the gentry and the tourists. Guilds, although in some places formally abolished, remained strong in printing, the docks and the arsenals, where job opportunities were always tightly controlled (sometimes by labour bosses who were simply organized criminals) and often virtually hereditary. Industrial work, particularly in textiles, was also done by peasant women and children at home, on the 'putting-out' system. But Italy lacked coal and had little iron, and these were huge handicaps in this early phase of industrialisation – imported coal cost six times the price in Britain. Cavour himself thought Italy could never become an industrial country, except in silk production and food processing.

The only flourishing industries able to export most of the product were, in fact, very closely linked to agricultural products: silk spinning at Como from the Lombard mulberry trees, wine-making in Tuscany or Sicily, and cheese-making on the Lombard irrigated plains. These processing industries ensured that agriculture flourished too, and also encouraged wider banking and credit networks. The silk trade, in particular, was on a large scale: it employed 43,000 workers in Piedmont alone by 1840, and at least 70,000 in Lombardy [107 *p. 45*]. Above all, it turned landowners into businessmen, who sold their products in Lyons or London, and came back with the latest ideas. Even so, workers in these industries usually had several other sources of family income, which helped them to survive in recessions.

The picture of Italian industry in these years is that of 'proto-industrialization': slow technical innovation, increasing trade in a very few but significant sectors, and a gradual squeeze on traditional guilds and craftsmen. These craftsmen could not compete with domestic 'outworkers', let alone with factory products from abroad; they relied on protective tariffs being maintained. Engineering and shipbuilding in Naples also relied on protection, as did the textile and clothing industry, and it did not prevent a considerable growth in wine and sulphur exports. Free trade was perhaps a good idea for landowners and silk merchants, but it would have been disastrous for much of industry. Yet by the 1830s 'free trade' doctrines were becoming more fashionable. In Piedmont, Charles Albert reduced grain tariffs markedly (from ninety to thirty lire per tonne in 1834, and more later), lifted the ban on the export of raw silk, and signed commercial treaties with other countries. To general surprise, the state budget actually benefited from these moves. Even in Naples the traditional policy of protecting artisans was reduced in 1845, largely because of British pressure. It was not a popular move, and threw thousands of textile workers out of a job. Even less popular was the government effort in 1847 to abolish the salt and tobacco monopolies and the farmed-out collection of excise duties. This threatened thousands more 'jobs' in Naples, including those of smugglers and semi-private police guards, whom no government could afford to annoy. Austria and her Italian dependents remained firmly protectionist, perhaps wisely. In fact, other innovations were probably more important than tariff reductions. Savings banks, for example, spread rapidly in northern Italy from the 1820s, lending essentially for land purchases. They were the first challenge to the traditional sources of rural finance, moneylenders and local lawyers seeking dependent clients.

By the mid-1840s the Italian economy was clearly changing rapidly. The poor harvests of 1845 and 1846 caused much hardship and forced peasants to move into the towns in search of bread and alms. This, in turn, put stress on public order and state budgets. Because food was so expensive, people could not buy other things, so artisans found few buyers for their goods. The immediate crisis was soon resolved by the good harvest of 1847, but it all contributed to the political upheaval of 1848.

More significant still were the long-term changes. New roads and canals were linking the various regions together. Above all, the railway age had arrived, creating new trading opportunities, perhaps even the prospect of Italy becoming again, for the first time in centuries, the route to the East. Now that the new Suez route was open, Italian railways, from Naples northwards, might carry the traffic between Asia and north-west Europe; they would be far quicker than the long sea route via Gibraltar. But the Austrians showed little interest in these possibilities. They insisted Lombard trade should use Trieste, not Genoa, nor even Venice, and in the 1850s refused to link Lombardy-Venetia by rail with either Turin or Genoa. The Lombards, a trading people, were furious, particularly as Austria was not a member of the German *Zollverein** and trade with her was in decline. In 1848 Lombardy had only two lines, one from Milan to the royal palace at Monza, the other to Treviglio on the route to Venice. Charles Albert, on the other hand, was busy with schemes linking Genoa to Savoy, France and Germany, many of which were constructed, or at least begun, in the 1850s. By this time it was clear that railways would transform the Italian economy, by hugely amplifying the potential market; and it was also clear that government support was essential. Or, at least, it was clear to men like Camillo di Cavour, who in the 1840s was personally active as an agent providing the rails for the Turin-Genoa line, as well as in helping to found banks to fund the operation [105, ii, *pp. 116–19*].

The campaign for railways was political as well as economic. Railways needed a common gauge, co-ordinated timetables and so forth. They also ensured that the host of existing customs barriers – seven, for example, from Lucca to Bologna – would seem even more ludicrous: trains could not keep stopping every few miles. In Germany, the *Zollverein* had proved a success from 1834; in Britain, the Corn Laws were abolished, and Cobden made a triumphal tour of Italy in 1847. Italy could not be left behind. And so a Customs League was proposed for Italy (see p. 48). Like the European Community over a century later, a Customs League needed not only common tariffs but also common weights and measures, common regulatory bodies and perhaps a common currency. It might even grow into a political union. However, these ambitious ideas were mostly restricted, as yet, to a small if growing group of optimistic intellectuals, economists and landowners. Many established commercial and industrial interests relied on state support and were usually grimly protectionist; they had little interest in railways, and lacked the imagination to see what they might bring.

5 PLOTS AND PATRIOTS

SECRET SOCIETIES AND INSURRECTIONS

After 1815 secret societies still flourished. There were many different sects, of varying views: e.g. *Calderari, Concistoriali, Guelfi,* and the *Adelfi,* who in 1818 became known as the Perfect Sublime Masters, led by the veteran revolutionary Filippo Buonarroti and influential in northern Italy. The most significant of all were the *Carbonari* (charcoal-burners), who attracted thousands of ex-Napoleonic officers and officials. By 1820 there were as many as 300,000 *Carbonari,* half of them in the mainland South. With such numbers the societies could be secret only in name. They had their own solemn oaths and initiation rites, and between seven and nine grades of membership: you learned the true purpose of the organization only on reaching the top grade. Most of their activities were charitable. They were local societies, influential in provincial towns among professional men, small landowners and artisans; and they differed much among themselves on social and political issues. Yet they adhered vaguely to the ideal of Italian independence from foreign rule, to constitutional liberties (for instance in the form of the Spanish Constitution of 1812) and even to Italian unity, at least in a federal or confederal form. They were much feared by the paranoid Restoration governments, and blamed for every sign of unrest [92, 100].

But as revolutionary organizations the *Carbonari* were only temporarily successful. They had members in the provincial administration and even in the garrisons of Naples itself. In July 1820 some of the *Carbonari*-inspired officers in Naples rose in revolt, inspired by the Spanish revolution earlier that year. They demanded, and briefly secured, a constitution. A new government was appointed, and it included some moderate *Carbonari.* But the *Carbonari* were faction-ridden, had no agreed policies and failed to mobilize support from elsewhere. Indeed, when the Palermo artisans rose in revolt too, demanding a Sicilian parliament and virtual independence, the new government in Naples sent an army led by the *Carbonarist* General

Pepe to suppress them; *Carbonari* from Messina and Catania joined Pepe in the fight. In March 1821 the Austrian army moved into Naples, the *Carbonari* government collapsed and the constitution was rescinded. As the Austrians attacked Naples, a group of aristocratic officers in Piedmont decided to act. They, too, demanded a constitution, and war against Austria for Italian 'independence'. King Victor Emanuel I decided to abdicate rather than give in; the future king, Charles Albert, acting as regent in Turin, did grant a constitution until, again, the Austrians put on military pressure.

These revolts showed that Restoration regimes were vulnerable. They could just about cope with student revolts or artisan risings in the towns, and they could largely ignore peasant unrest. But the real danger came from palace coups, from officers in the elite army corps stationed in the capital cities. Such officers were quite likely to be in the secret societies; they were strongly influenced by heroic risings abroad; and their coups were quite likely to succeed. However, the Austrians would soon restore the previous regime. Restoration governments had few reliable troops of their own; but they did have the Austrian army available in time of need. This was a trump card. The regimes may have been weak, but the opposition was weaker still. This fact was rarely recognized by governments, and never admitted by the revolutionaries.

In 1830–1 came more revolts, triggered by the July Days of 1830 in Paris, and by the risings in Flanders and Poland. In December 1830 riots broke out in Rome, during a Papal Conclave; and soon local risings took place all over Papal Emilia-Romagna, as well as in the duchies of Parma and Modena. The Duke of Modena even encouraged these revolts for a time, in the hope of winning more territory. Eventually the Romagna insurgents decided to march on Rome, but the new Pope, Gregory XVI, appealed to the Catholic Powers. The Austrian army yet again restored order, and brought back the duchies' rulers. Austrian troops stayed on in Bologna until 1838, and the French maintained a garrison at Ancona.

MAZZINI AND 'YOUNG ITALY'

The failures of the secret societies in Emilia-Romagna in 1830–31 persuaded one young Genoese *Carbonaro*, the lawyer Giuseppe Mazzini, that secret societies could not bring about the Italian revolution, and that the French could not be relied on to support it. Italy would have to 'go it alone' (*fare da sè*). In October 1831, while in exile in Marseilles, he founded 'Young Italy' – 'young' because people over forty were not allowed to join. 'Young Italy' was itself initially organized much like the old conspiratorial societies, and it concentrated on local issues, such as jobs for laymen in the Romagna Legations, just as they had done. But Mazzini soon began to aim at a mass political movement, with 'national' aims and dedicated to organizing mass insurrection. In short, he thought in terms of an Italian national party, aiming to take over political power from all the existing states and to found a new regime.

Mazzini was a superbly gifted journalist and prophet rather than a man of action. His journal, also called *Young Italy*, was more influential than his party. He took for granted that an 'Italian nation' existed, based on a common (literary) culture; this 'nation', like the other European nations, had the right to self-government and independence. The existing Italian states should be replaced by a unitary republic imbued with the (French) principles of equality and participation. However, he was willing to accept kingly contributions to the cause of independence, and in 1831 wrote a famous letter to King Charles Albert of Piedmont, urging him to take the lead in driving the Austrians from the peninsula, bringing in free institutions and becoming king of a united Italy. Charles Albert, who was trying to negotiate an alliance with the Austrians at the time, took no notice. Mazzini's real enemy was the Papacy. His followers were anticlerical as well as insurrectionary. Most of them wanted a secular Italy, with compulsory lay education and lay welfare, and Rome as its capital. This meant not only the end of the Pope's Temporal Power, but the end of the papacy's spiritual dominance over the Italian people. Mazzini himself believed firmly in God, took for granted that God favoured Italian unity, and preached the austere virtues of a 'civil religion', all duty and devotion to the people [69, 77].

Mazzini, therefore, advocated a new trinity: independence, unity, and liberty. His was an 'aggregating' nationalism – the various existing Italian states should be joined together. They should, in his view, include Corsica, Malta, the South Tyrol and probably also the canton of Ticino in Switzerland, for all were Italian-speaking and shared the same culture. Indeed, Mazzini was the prophet only of 'big-nation nationalism'. There should be, at most, a dozen nation-states in Europe. He had no time for separatists in peripheral areas like Sicily or Ireland, nor even for established states like Portugal and Denmark. As for Sicily and Sardinia, they were simply Italian – their inhabitants had no separate cultural traditions of their own – and he was not even prepared to countenance dual identity, 'Sicilian' and 'Italian'. He also disliked 'federalist' or 'confederalist' proposals, and normally (but not always) advocated a single unitary republic, with a written constitution and universal suffrage.

And how was all this to be achieved? Mazzini's answer was popular insurrection, a people's guerrilla on the Spanish model, which would overthrow foreign domination and domestic tyrants alike. Like all revolutionaries, he believed that people detested their existing governments and were eagerly awaiting the signal to depose them. Just one more landing on a remote southern beach would surely explode the whole system. Hence he spent many years fomenting and organizing revolts and insurrections. None of them was successful – and if any of them had been, the Austrians would have moved in. In 1833 the police in Genoa uncovered quite a widespread conspiracy against Charles Albert. In 1834 Mazzini organized an invasion of Savoy by 223 men under the ex-Napoleonic general Ramorino; it ended in predictable disaster. Undeterred, he and his followers continued their efforts. 'Young Italy' was not, of course, alone. The *Carbonari* were still strong in the south, as were other societies like the *Filadelfi* or Nicola Fabrizi's Italic Legion. Each sect had its own programme and its own blueprint for the Italian future. There were also more or less freelance revolutionaries like the Bandiera brothers, two Venetian officers serving in the Austrian navy: they founded their own secret society, *Esperia*, in 1840, and in 1844 landed in Calabria and proclaimed the republic, to no avail. Many of the 'revolutionaries' were strong on rhetoric but very reluctant to act; others were only interested in local issues, like seizing some more Church land. Those few who did lead insurrections found little support, particularly in distant regions where they could not even understand the dialect. Mazzini usually opposed other people's projects, but his own were no more successful [43, 77, 115] [*Doc. 3*].

By the mid-1840s Mazzini's schemes were widely derided, even in conspiratorial circles. Critics accused him of despatching successive waves of hopeful insurgents to their useless deaths year after year, while he himself sat safely in Switzerland or London. No Restoration government had been brought down, despite manifest popular unrest. In any case, the Austrian police had cracked 'Young Italy's code, and knew who subscribed to the journal. It was clear that Mazzini's whole strategy was futile. He wrote constantly of 'the people', but as an exile knew little about them. Indeed, 'the people', in Mazzinian parlance, meant the urban, literate people: independent artisans and craftsmen, together with students, lawyers and the occasional lesser nobleman impressed by Mazzini's ideas. It deliberately excluded the mass of the population, not only the peasants but also the urban 'plebs', too poor and ignorant to be trusted. A genuine 'people's war' of the Spanish or Greek kind would have meant mobilizing the real people, the peasantry; and that would have meant winning over the clergy, whom the revolutionaries detested. Alternatively, a strategy of non-violent resistance might well have been more effective, and indeed in the form of a tobacco strike it did trigger revolt in Milan in 1848; but somehow the upright, moralistic Mazzini never advocated it.

Yet Italian unification turned out to owe a great deal to Mazzini. For thirty years he inspired successive generations of idealistic students and artisans. He had few committed followers and was distrusted even by most of them, but he was admired by many from afar, and feared by governments. Rulers were not so secure, nor so confident of their subjects' loyalty, that they could ignore their archcritic. Mazzini's strategy was preposterous, his knowledge of Italy minimal, his practical impact (until 1848) negligible. Yet he helped to undermine the legitimacy of Italy's rulers, and to legitimise instead the process of unification. By advocating republican liberty, rule by the sovereign people and universal suffrage, he linked unity to freedom and to democracy. He explained why a united Italy was morally desirable, and did it in 'modern', 'European' terms, not in romantic or ethnic ones. Like most political schemes, Italian unification needed to be propelled along by a gigantic output of rhetoric. But it had to be the right kind of rhetoric: populist, militarist and uplifting. Mazzini provided this, over a lifetime. His was a voice crying in the wilderness. Most people ignored him, but they could never be quite sure that he might not turn out to be right.

'MODERATE' PATRIOTISM

Mazzini was influential because similar, if less unrealistic, ideas were already widespread in Italian intellectual circles. From the 1790s onwards there had been much resentment of foreign domination, and also a sense that society could be restructured along progressive, egalitarian lines. 'Nationalist' ideas grew up, after 1815, from this fertile soil. In Italy, unlike Germany, they were not a reaction against French ideas, but an offshoot of them. Although the occasional poet like Alfieri turned against French 'cosmopolitanism', there was never a real revolt in Italy against the Enlightenment. 'National' ideas remained 'progressive' and appealed to the same type of urban, literate people who had been most influenced by the French. Another characteristic feature of Italian nationalism was that most 'moderate' patriots wanted 'independence', freedom from foreign rule, much more than they wanted 'unity'. The existence of the Papal States in central Italy seemed an insuperable obstacle to any hope of forming a single Italian state, at least unless that state were to be 'federal' or 'confederal' in kind. Mazzini, who rejected federalism and was quite willing to tackle the Papacy, was an exception. Most Italians recognized that Italy was a very diverse country, and that her institutions should reflect the varied histories and cultures of different parts of the peninsula.

Still, at least the Italian 'moderate' patriots did not have to invent a glorious past, as their counterparts elsewhere often did. It really existed, and the evidence, in this golden age of archaeology, was being further revealed every day. Nationalists could point to the ancient Romans – of the republic, of course, rather than the empire – as models of civil virtue and effective statecraft; to the medieval popes, communes and *signorie*, which had resisted invading German emperors; and to the Renaissance, which had spread Italian ideas and culture throughout the civilized world. In the 1830s and 1840s a profusion of historical works appeared. Most of them were regional and antiquarian, but they had an implied message: these regions were all part of 'Italy', and 'Italy' had fought successfully against foreign invaders in the past. The Sicilian historian Michele Amari, for example, wrote a famous book in 1841 on the medieval revolt known as the Sicilian Vespers: it denounced sectarian plotting, but showed what could be achieved by a popular insurrection. Historical novels – especially Alessandro Manzoni's enormously successful *I Promessi Sposi* (*The Betrothed*) – spread much the same implied message, to a wider audience. So did opera. Rossini's *William Tell* depicted the successful Swiss struggle against the Habsburgs. Verdi's *Nabucco*, with its famous 'Chorus of the Hebrew Slaves', had an even stronger appeal.

However, Italian national sentiment was perhaps essentially linguistic rather than historical. It depended on the glories of the Italian language, and of Italian literature. Dante became the 'national poet', the genius who had created 'Italian' as a literary language known to all educated Italians and many educated Europeans. All literate people throughout the country were likely to know long passages of Dante by heart. There was no argument, in Italy, about which dialect should become the official language: Dante had settled that in the fourteenth century. Every time an Italian picked up a book or a newspaper, he was reminded of his cultural identity. It was a vital common bond among the educated. However, very few people actually spoke Italian – only around 2.5 per cent of the population, mostly in Tuscany and Rome; the rest spoke local dialects, incomprehensible to people elsewhere. The use of Italian thus became a political symbol. Many of those who did not speak Italian felt that they should do so. In 1844, for example, the Piedmontese agrarian association banned the use of dialect at its meetings, although most farmers spoke nothing else, because the Italian language was 'patrimony and bond between all inhabitants of Italy' [105, ii, *p. 95*]. Cavour himself had to learn Italian as his third language (and purists complained that he never mastered it). In 1852 came the ultimate accolade, when the University of Turin decided that lectures should henceforth be given in Italian, rather than Latin.

Italian national sentiment, therefore, could draw on a glorious history and a strong linguistic and literary 'high culture' as a major part of the European heritage. These were huge advantages. However, municipal and regional identity remained stronger than any 'national' sentiment. Belli's poems in the Roman dialect were very successful; even Manzoni's *Promessi Sposi* was originally written in Milanese. Furthermore, to be 'Italian', or even to speak Italian, was to be educated and sophisticated. Like the Mazzinians, the 'moderate' patriots knew little, and cared little, about the vast majority of Italy's real inhabitants. Unlike nationalists elsewhere, they noticeably failed to investigate or glorify the folk culture or popular traditions of the Italian countryside. Perhaps only on the islands of Sardinia (Spano) and Sicily (Pitrè) were there scholars anxious to show the importance of local folk cultures. Elsewhere the peasants were ignored, or feared: they spoke no Italian, they were irredeemably superstitious, and they had never heard of 'Italy'.

I should stress that national 'identity', where it existed at all, did not necessarily imply 'nationalism', i.e. any demand for a new political structure. The Italian language, esteemed though it was, defined a cultural community, not a would-be political one. Hence it was possible for the Austrians to encourage 'Italian' cultural initiatives like the founding of the *Biblioteca Italiana*, an important Italian-language periodical, in 1816. Its editor, Giuseppe Acerbi, was no nationalist. He took the very Milanese view that Milan was Italy's only centre of cultural excellence, and that this status rested on wise Austrian policies of promoting education. Many well-known scholars, such as Melchiorre Gioia and Giandomenico Romagnosi, were happy to write for the *Biblioteca*. The Austrians had no objection either, at least until the 1840s, to literary or historical works in Italian; Massimo d'Azeglio published his historical novels in Lombardy, such as *Ettore Fieramosca* in 1833 [20].

Even so, writers and poets had their own personal motives for becoming 'nationalist' in the political sense. They needed a free market in books throughout Italy – but not too free. Books published in one Italian state were not copyright elsewhere, so publishers in the other seven states soon brought out pirate editions, which could be sold cheaper than the originals since the author received no royalties. And, of course, each state had its own censors, so a book freely on sale in one state might be seized and banned elsewhere. Moreover, the government in Naples imposed a high tariff on book imports in 1822. By the 1830s an all-Italian agreement on copyright, and free trade in works of literature, had become essential demands of the intellectual classes. The Austrian Chief Minister, Metternich, saw the need to give way. A copyright agreement was in fact signed in 1840, although not by Naples, but by then the damage had been done. A real gap had opened up between intellectuals and governments, worsened by the poor prospects of getting a government job.

In short, the sects and the Mazzinians were nothing like as important as they (and their opponents) supposed; but what did matter was the spread of moderate 'Italian' sentiment among respectable citizens. The 'scientific congresses', held annually from 1839 to 1847, each time in a different Italian state, were another striking example of this process. Modelled on the meetings of the British Association for the Advancement of Science, they provided a national forum for hundreds of Italian scientists, economists and academics to discuss progress in their fields. There was much stress on agriculture and geology, both sciences with practical, economic applications; and, above all, on medicine – over a third of the participants were medical specialists. In a sense they were 'European', bringing in ideas and innovations from abroad, but they also promoted a sense of being part of an Italian intellectual community, concerned with the same problems, reading the same journals and using the same language – a language in which modern scientific and technological issues could be discussed as easily as in French or German. And they discussed public policy issues, urged progressive reforms, debated them in quasi-parliamentary fashion and produced reports with explicitly political recommendations. They helped greatly to create an Italian intellectual elite and an Italian 'public opinion', no longer restricted to romantic poets or regional groupings but now embracing economists, bankers and farmers, men in touch with business, the army and the Courts. Many of the future heroes of the Risorgimento attended these congresses. They came to know and admire, even to trust, each other.

The congresses were not alone. The spread of newspapers and journals was vital, perhaps above all Carlo Cattaneo's highly informed and very liberal *Il Politecnico* in Milan (1839–45). Between 1842 and

1847 the first *Popular Encyclopaedia*, modelled on its Glasgow namesake, was published in Italy. Soon it had 5000 subscribers. It was very science-oriented and tended to avoid contemporary controversies, but its implied message was clear: the sum of human knowledge could be acquired, in Italian. And, of course, there were a host of other meeting-places, where new ideas could be discussed – clubs, freemasonry (banned after 1815 but still prominent in many provincial centres), agrarian associations, public banquets (a great opportunity for speech-making), even cafes and theatres. Above all, there was a great deal of detailed and well-informed debate, in pamphlets, learned journals and the press, on the key social and economic issues of the day. Prisons, welfare, sanitation, child labour, pauperism, prostitution, schooling, railways – all these topics were treated by numerous writers, many of them later to become prominent politicians. Here, too, we can see the formation of an Italian 'public opinion'. And informed debate could easily become a demand for informed decision-making, and for a share in that decision-making [88 *pp. 108–10*] [*Doc. 4*].

National sentiment thus became more evident in the 1830s and 1840s. It was often linked to the long-established demand for a constitution, and to the more recent fashion for 'liberal' reforms of all kinds – a free press, free trade, popular education and so forth. It was first expressed clearly in Florence in the 1820s by Gian Pietro Vieusseux' mostly literary journal *Antologia*, which advocated national emancipation via liberal reforms, which would ultimately achieve the goal of an Italian federation. And then there was Silvio Pellico's famous book *Le Mie Prigioni* (*My Prisons*) (1832), describing his life in the Austrian prison of Spielberg, a work that hugely damaged Austria's reputation for efficient government. Railways contributed to this shift in opinion; so did the difficulties of Lombard merchants wanting to use Genoa rather than Trieste; so did the successful example of Louis Philippe's France. 'Liberal' propagandists wanted reforms, not revolution; 'federalism', not 'unity'. They were prepared to work within existing states, and wait for Austrian power to weaken. Nor were there many countervailing anti-liberal voices among writers and journalists. The dynastic principle had few adherents, and devout Catholics were often progressive and 'national' too.

In this atmosphere an exiled Piedmontese priest, Vincenzo Gioberti, published in 1843 a famous programme for Italian 'unification', *Del Primato Morale e Civile degli Italiani* (*On the Moral and Civil Primacy of the Italians*). Gioberti was no Mazzinian, indeed he thought Mazzini should be confined to a lunatic asylum, and that ' "Young

Italy" has done more harm to our country than all the despots that have oppressed her' [43 *p. 388*]. Gioberti started from the premiss that the existing Italian states were a reality, unlike 'the people'. Just as Vieusseux had done twenty years earlier, he argued that Italy should be 'unified' by means of a confederation of states, under the nominal leadership of the Pope. The confederation could establish internal free trade, common weights, measures and currency, and agree on other issues as need arose. This 'neo-guelph'* programme, deliberately recalling medieval precedents, had a huge impact – although, being over 800 pages long and not divided into chapters, one may doubt if it was much read. It appeared to offer the benefits of 'unification' without posing any threat to existing sovereigns, and without any need for unpleasant events like war, revolution or foreign intervention. Pope Pius IX, elected in 1846, was clearly influenced by Gioberti (see p. 47). But the *Primacy* had serious flaws, as soon became apparent. It did not mention the Austrians, who would presumably remain in control of Lombardy-Venetia and dominant elsewhere. Moreover, papal authority in temporal matters was not effective in central Italy and was not likely to be accepted anywhere else either. His book reflected the views of moderate northern Catholics, keen to preserve local traditions and very hostile to the prospect of a centralized state of the old French type.

The next year, partly as a response to Gioberti, came Cesare Balbo's *Le Speranze d'Italia* (*The Hopes of Italy*). Balbo was also Piedmontese, but his family had long served the state, and he knew something of international politics. He argued for a federal Italy, also based on the existing states but led by Piedmont, not the Papacy. Charles Albert would have to take the initiative. Piedmont would take over Lombardy, and the Austrians would be compensated with ex-Turkish lands in the Balkans. This, in his view, could easily be secured by international diplomacy, without any need for war. Balbo wanted Italian 'independence'; he did not worry too much about unity, nor about liberty – he did not envisage an Italian parliament, nor even reforms in the various states. Indeed, 'Italy' seemed to mean essentially Piedmont and Lombardy. But his book had an even bigger impact than Gioberti's. It obviously reflected official Piedmontese ambitions, and enjoyed Charles Albert's approval. Both Balbo and Gioberti were gradualists, both as regards 'unity' and 'liberty'. And they both ignored the obvious objection: what would happen when Austria said no?

Other works followed, particularly Massimo d'Azeglio's *Degli Ultimi Casi di Romagna* (*On Recent Events in the Romagna*) (1846), written at the express suggestion of Charles Albert to preach the 'moderate' cause even among the misruled *Romagnoli*. A 'neo-ghibelline'* school (Niccolini, Amari, Giuseppe La Farina) appeared, in reaction to Gioberti, celebrating the anti-papal, lay tradition of Machiavelli, Sarpi and the Enlightenment. Similar views were some-times expressed by liberal Catholic reformers, hostile to the papacy's Temporal Power and opposed to anything that might reinforce it. Despite these differences, the real point is that by the mid-1840s the future of Italy was being actively debated by 'moderate' writers, mostly Piedmontese aristocrats but with some adherents in Lombardy and Tuscany. These men were optimistic, liberal and anxious for peaceful change. Or, to put it another way, the 'Mazzinian' revol-utionaries had become discredited, and the Piedmontese 'moderates' were upstaging them by developing national political programmes.

In short, 'national sentiment', now quite widespread among the elite, was turning into quasi-'nationalist' political demands. Admit-tedly it was all very tentative as yet, but Charles Albert was clearly involved, and the economic incentives were becoming stronger by the day. These political demands were not just 'Italian', they were 'Euro-pean' in nature, embracing constitutional government, representative institutions, free trade, railways and state education. By the 1840s there was a 'moderate' political grouping, with royal support in Piedmont, which was committed to political change and to rejecting Austrian rule. It all amounted to what d'Azeglio, in a famous phrase, called 'a conspiracy of public opinion in broad daylight' [42, i, *p. 319*]: a conspiracy to mobilize men's minds, not to lead an insurrection.

6 THE REVOLUTIONS OF 1848

A TIME FOR CONSTITUTIONS

Yet in 1848 insurrections did occur, throughout Italy. Few had predicted them. True, living standards had been declining for at least two decades. The poor harvests of 1845 and 1846 had made matters a great deal worse, and doubled the price of bread. Urban artisans were hit by trade recession and (in Naples) by tariff reform. The professional classes suffered from poor job prospects and censorship, and businessmen complained about the slow expansion of the railways. But most of these grievances were not new, and the harvest of 1847 was good. There seemed to be no immediate political danger to the existing regimes. The Austrian army was intact; the Mazzinians were few, and discredited.

Yet three unexpected factors undermined the regimes. The first was a new pope. In June 1846 Giovanni Maria Mastai-Ferretti was elected pope, taking the name of Pius IX. Coming straight from his diocese of Imola in the Romagna, he realised the need for reforms. Within a month he issued an amnesty to political prisoners, and hundreds returned to the Papal States from exile. Laymen were admitted to a larger role in government and the courts, taxes were reduced and press censorship relaxed. In 1847 an advisory Council of State was set up, with representatives from each province. Moreover, he founded a civic guard, long a republican demand and soon infiltrated by republicans. Pius not only brought in more open government in his own states, he was clearly influenced by 'neo-guelph' ideas and seemed personally sympathetic to the 'Italian' – i.e. anti-Austrian – cause in northern Italy.

There was much popular enthusiasm for all this. Pius became a national hero, making the 'national' cause legitimate. Even Mazzini wrote to him, urging him to lead the campaign for Italian rights. In short, he seemed a 'liberal Pope', in Metternich's horrified phrase – although this was, of course, never true. Metternich hastily reinforced the Austrian garrison at Ferrara and occupied the city itself, within the Papal States. Here was a real challenge to papal authority. Pius retaliated subtly. He proposed a customs league, on the model of the German *Zollverein*: goods should be traded freely throughout the peninsula, without any internal tariffs. This was, on the face of it, irresistible. Tuscany and (with some reluctance) Piedmont agreed to join. Early in November 1847 a treaty was signed. It envisaged not merely a customs league but an eventual 'federation', with a diet (parliament) in Rome 'harmonizing' weights and measures and even exerting powers over foreign policy and defence. Gioberti's ideal was, it seemed, being realized: an Italian confederation, or even federation, under papal leadership. But the Austrian-held territories were left out in the cold, as they were from the *Zollverein*. The league therefore implied, or threatened, an end to automatic Austrian dominance of Italian economic and political life. If successful, the Lombards and Venetians would certainly have agitated strongly to join it, whatever their Austrian rulers thought. Moreover, in the Pope's view it also made an Italian 'national' war against Austria less likely. The Austrians might fight against insurrectionaries or against Piedmont, but they could hardly make war on trade.

If the Pope could bring in reforms, how could the other rulers resist? In autumn 1847 both Leopold II in Tuscany and Charles Albert in Piedmont astonished their subjects with new 'liberal' legislation. In Piedmont, press censorship was virtually lifted, and a host of new journals – including one called the *Risorgimento*, edited by Balbo and Camillo di Cavour – suddenly appeared. Elected provincial and municipal councils were set up, court procedure was made public and freedom of association proclaimed. Charles Albert's benevolence did not impress the Genoese, who rioted early in 1848 (against the Jesuits), but it had unexpected consequences in remote Sardinia. A delegation set out from the island asking for similar treatment and especially for access to the customs league – much of Sardinian trade was with Tuscany and the Papal States. In return, the Sardinians would give up their own laws and administrative system altogether, and enter a 'perfect fusion' with the mainland kingdom. They would thus become, for the first time, subject to Piedmontese taxes and Piedmontese laws, including conscription. On 30 November 1847 the delegation's request was granted, by a bemused monarch. This was the first 'voluntary' annexation of the Risorgimento (Liguria had been allocated to Piedmont in 1814 by the Powers). It was a harbinger of what better trade prospects, and liberal-sounding institutions promising political liberties, might achieve: a voluntary act of union, a merger of different regions into one kingdom, with uniform (Piedmontese) laws and a uniform (Piedmontese) administration.

The second major factor undermining the existing states was that in 1847 civil war broke out in Switzerland. The Catholic *Sonderbund* attempted to retain their cantonal independence within a weak confederation; but their opponents won. By 1848 Switzerland had a new 'federal' constitution, with guaranteed civil rights, popular democracy and some degree of central authority on economic, foreign and military affairs. The lesson was not lost on northern Italy. The Swiss, after all, had once been subject to Austrian rule themselves. They had thrown it off in the Middle Ages, and now they had successfully founded a workable, liberal regime. In Milan, in particular, just a few miles from the Swiss border, men looked wistfully northwards and sought to emulate their democratic neighbours.

Thirdly, it was clear that Austria was unusually weak. The Italian situation in the 1840s was rather like that of eastern Europe in the 1980s. A major outside Power imposed much internal policy, guaranteed the stability of the various regimes and suppressed the occasional revolt, with the tacit consent of rival states. Yet that Power was greatly over-extended, and much weaker than she had been twenty years earlier. In the case of Austria, the emperor, Ferdinand I, was mentally handicapped and her government increasingly ineffective. She had no money and few reliable troops. Her concerns were predominantly in central and eastern Europe, to which northern Italy was irrelevant except inasmuch as it provided one-third of the imperial revenues. Austria thus needed Lombardy-Venetia for its taxes, but she could not afford to defend it properly, let alone to finance adequate public works. Moreover, the new pope's proclamations were having a real impact on the Lombard and Venetian clergy, and hence on the peasantry; and there was also a new Archbishop of Milan, an 'Italian' sympathizer. Without the support of Church or peasantry, the Austrians were in trouble. French power was reviving too, and Charles Albert was clearly spoiling for a fight. Austria was dangerously isolated. Her main ally, Britain, was distinctly unreliable on the Italian question: the British were soft on Piedmont and were active propagandists for liberalism. A British government emissary, Lord Minto, proceeded solemnly round Italy in 1847–8, preaching the benefits of constitutional government to the benighted natives. He visited Charles Albert and Pius IX, telling them what they should do to be saved. With allies like that, thought Metternich, who needed enemies?

Early in January 1848, tired of futile petitions asking for civil liberties and autonomy, the canny Milanese began a novel form of protest. The Austrian taxes on tobacco and on the lottery, which brought in five million lire a year to the imperial coffers, could be avoided by the cunning expedient of not smoking or gambling. Here was an Italian version of the Boston Tea Party, as disastrous for state finances then as it would be now. The tobacco boycott was organized originally by disaffected young aristocrats at the Jockey Club, and soon spread to other cities, and to Venetia. Austrian soldiers retaliated by smoking ostentatiously in public, and were then attacked by passers-by. The tobacco boycott was a difficult tactic to combat: people could hardly be forced to smoke. In Milan, tension soon grew acute, unsoothed by nicotine. Six people were killed in disturbances. On 25 February the Austrians declared martial law over all Lombardy and Venetia.

Meanwhile in Sicily a popular rising took place in the major cities on 12 January, demanding that the 1812 Constitution be restored, although without a hereditary upper house. Ferdinand II, in Naples, offered the Sicilians 'autonomy', and proposed an 'Orleanist'* parliament instead, for both Sicily and the mainland. This was accepted in Naples, where elections were soon held to the new assembly, but rejected in Sicily. The Sicilians, in fact, soon set up a provisional government of their own, a mixture of (mostly) aristocratic 'moderates' and 'democrats'. This government's main task was to maintain, or rather to restore, public order; it set up a National Guard of property-owners to contain the lower orders. It was distinctly hostile to Naples, was totally unmoved by any nationalist rhetoric about Italian unity, and was determined that all government posts in Sicily should be reserved in future for Sicilians. For a few months Sicily remained independent, and in July a new, more 'advanced' constitution was proclaimed: the lower house of parliament was to have most power, and was to be elected on the basis of literacy not property. But in September Ferdinand's troops moved in and abolished the new regime; the king's famous nickname 'King Bomba' was acquired in this campaign, when he ordered the artillery bombardment of Messina. Thereafter Sicily, still resentful and insurrectionary, was brought under military rule and remained aloof from the later tempests of 1848–9.

Once Ferdinand of Naples had granted a liberal constitution, rulers elsewhere had to follow suit – in Tuscany on 11 February, in Piedmont on 4 March. Charles Albert was, in fact, very reluctant to do so. He had sworn an oath back in 1823 not to grant a constitution; faced with irresistible pressure, he thought of abdicating until the Archbishop of Vercelli thoughtfully released him from his promise.

Even so, the new Piedmontese Constitution – the famous *Statuto*, which remained formally in force until 1947 – made few concessions to 'democracy'. The elected Chamber of Deputies had a property-based franchise, so less than 2 per cent of the population had the vote; the upper house, or Senate, consisted of life peers appointed by the king. The king retained many other prerogative powers, including a formal veto on legislation and a by no means formal right to make war and peace. Still, it may not have been particularly democratic, but it did guarantee civil rights, and it was a constitution. Pius IX in Rome also promised, on 14 March, a two-chamber legislative assembly, the lower one to be elected, although its decisions might be overruled by the College of Cardinals. Laymen should henceforth be a majority on Rome's civil government.

All this was fairly peaceful. True, there had been an insurrection in Sicily, and the tobacco boycott continued in Milan, but in Naples, Florence, Turin and Rome liberal constitutions promising civil liberties, a free press and an elected assembly were promulgated, with the support of all respectable opinion and the blessing of the Church. Admittedly they were promulgated lest worse befall – worse being, to liberals and absolutist rulers alike, a 'popular' revolution of a democratic-republican kind. Most of the Italian states, including the Papacy, thus became constitutional monarchies almost overnight. Governments continued to be run by 'moderate' ministers. There were no insurrections on the Italian mainland, and no need for them. People continued to trust that the new Customs League might develop into a federal political union, perhaps now including the Two Sicilies.

INSURRECTIONS AND WAR

In Lombardy-Venetia the Austrians refused to grant reforms. But revolt broke out in Vienna, and on 13 March Metternich fell. This was too good an opportunity to miss. The Milanese and Venetians rose on 18 March, proclaiming the usual liberal demands and the end of Austrian rule. The insurgents in Milan fought heroically for five days against the Austrian garrison of 12,000 men. They were mostly unarmed artisans (blacksmiths, joiners and the like), and were strongly backed by the archbishop: at least 100 priests fought on the barricades, and the bust of Pius IX was hoisted on them. By 20 March much of the surrounding countryside had risen too, cutting the Austrians off from their supplies. Austrian food and ammunition began to run low, and the Piedmontese were expected to intervene. The

Austrian commander, Radetzky, therefore decided to withdraw from the city, and moved his army to the stronghold forts of the Lombard-Venetian 'Quadrilateral'* (Peschiera-Verona-Legnago-Mantua). It looked like a sudden, astonishing collapse of the Austrian regime. Radetzky could not, in fact, rely on the loyalty of most of his troops: 24 of his 61 infantry battalions consisted of Italian conscripts, and a further nine were Hungarians sympathetic to the Italian cause. The local inhabitants plied them with drink and encouraged them to desert. Nor could Radetzky hope for reinforcements, since the Vienna government was virtually bankrupt and beset with problems elsewhere. But he could, and did, hold out in the Quadrilateral fortresses, and from there he even managed to reconquer much of Venetia [110].

In Milan and Venice provisional governments took over, mostly the usual aristocrats and landowners, brought to power by artisan revolt. They proclaimed the usual civil liberties. Then came a dilemma. Should they proclaim a republic, or 'Italian unity'? In Venice, more remote from Austrian troops and with a glorious republican tradition, the (Venetian) Republic was proclaimed; in Milan it was not. Cattaneo and his influential group of 'democrats' argued for a Milanese republic, to become part of an Italian federation later; but the provisional government of Count Casati hesitated. It had no troops and weapons available; it feared losing control of the situation, to the 'democrats' and insurrectionaries; and it knew the Austrians would fight back. Unwilling to proclaim a republic, and lacking a king of their own, the Lombard 'moderates' turned to Charles Albert, and to the regular Piedmontese army, to defend them.

Charles Albert needed little prompting. Proclaiming that Italy would 'go it alone' (*fare da sè*) – a phrase indicating that French help was not welcome – he invaded Lombardy on 24 March. He did so not to help the Milanese against the Austrians, nor to proclaim a liberal constitution in Milan, nor to prevent a revolution there, nor to forestall the French, nor even to save his dynasty from possible revolt at home. He invaded in order to annex the whole of Lombardy (at least) to Piedmont, with the willing consent of its rulers, and while the Austrians were not in a position to resist. True, the Lombard 'moderates' did insist on a plebiscite being held to ratify the 'fusion'; 550,000 out of 650,000 voters approved it. They also secured the promise of a 'Constituent Assembly', to draft a new constitution for the new extended monarchy. But this was just to save face. The reality was that the heroic 'democratic' rising in Milan had led only to Charles Albert annexing Lombardy. Cattaneo, who thought he was a worse tyrant than the Austrians, was furious.

The Piedmontese invasion of Austrian territory turned the Lombard protest movement into full-scale conventional war, to be fought mainly by regular armies. But 'national sentiment' was extremely important too. Other Italian states, particularly Tuscany and Naples, sent troops to help fight off the inevitable Austrian counter-attack. Even the Papal army, with 12,000 volunteers including two of the Pope's nephews, joined in: its commander, General Durando, was sent north to defend the Papal frontiers against the Austrians, but on 21 April crossed the Po into Lombardy, without authorization. Moreover, thousands of Habsburg troops had deserted, at least partly through sympathy; whereas the various Italian armies were all swollen by thousands of 'volunteers', irregular troops of eager enthusiasts. Even Charles Albert, crossing the frontier into Lombardy, proclaimed he was acting in the name of 'Italy'. This was not just rhetoric, to conceal his dynastic ambition; it rang true to many patriots, at least for a time [*Doc. 5*].

The conventional war turned out, unexpectedly, to be an unequivocal victory for the Austrians. Despite nominal support from the other Italian states, Charles Albert could not prise Radetzky's troops out of the Quadrilateral, although he did take Peschiera in May. The Piedmontese army despised its badly-armed Lombard allies, distrusted the republican Venetians even more, and had little time for disreputable volunteers from other regions. In turn, the volunteers distrusted Charles Albert, who was obviously more bent on organizing plebiscites and annexations than on defeating the Austrians. Indeed, it was clear by summer 1848 that Charles Albert did not want to fight at all, and was assuming that French or British diplomatic pressure would give him Lombardy without a real war. In this he was much mistaken.

When Austria finally managed to send reinforcements over the Brenner, Radetzky emerged from his forts and defeated the Piedmontese at the battle of Custoza, on 25 July. He then re-entered Milan on 6 August, meeting negligible resistance, although almost a third of the population fled the city with the retreating Piedmontese army. This was the end of the Lombardy rising. It was noticeable that Milan, and Lombardy generally, played little part in later agitations and insurrections, even in 1859–60. Charles Albert had alienated the Lombard peasantry with his taxes and conscription, and he had offered them very little, not even the vote. Even so, most landowners and clergy remained anti-Austrian after 1848; thereafter Lombardy had to be ruled by the army.

Thereafter there were rather feeble diplomatic efforts to settle the Austro-Piedmontese war. Since Radetzky had won, he saw no reason to concede any territory; nor did the French or British have sufficient incentive to persuade him otherwise. In March 1849 Charles Albert tried again, hoping (in vain) for another Lombard insurrection. Radetzky again defeated him, at the battle of Novara on 23 March 1849. Defeated in war and unconvincing as a peacetime constitutional monarch, Charles Albert abdicated the Piedmontese throne, and died four months later. Radetzky imposed lenient armistice terms, perhaps to shore up a future 'conservative' regime in Piedmont under the new young king, Victor Emanuel II, or perhaps out of fear of French intervention. Piedmont had to pay 75 million lire to cover some of the costs of the war, and had to allow Austrian troops in the frontier town of Alessandria. It was an inglorious end to a national crusade.

In Venice, the Habsburgs had been disliked by virtually all classes, particularly the sailors and the workers in the Arsenal. When insurrection broke out, the Austrian troops surrendered without a shot, and the Republic was proclaimed on 22 March 1848 by Daniele Manin, a 'democratic' lawyer. Anti-Austrian risings succeeded in all the major towns except Verona, which remained in Radetzky's hands. But the conservative landowners of mainland Venetia (the *terraferma**) were less than delighted by this outcome, particularly when Manin's provisional government abolished the poll tax and reduced the price of salt by one-third. Soon the rural areas were retaken by Austrian reinforcements. Even in the city itself, the 'democrats' were divided. Were they fighting to restore the *Serenissima**, an oligarchy if ever there was one? Or should they join with the Lombards and the Piedmontese, in the anti-Austrian campaign? Or did they aspire to a 'democratic' Venetian Republic, linked to some sort of Italian federation or (by late 1848) to their republican colleagues in Rome? The answer, for some time, was: wait and see. Manin declared that once the war against Austria had been won (by others), then would be the time to discuss future constitutional arrangements. The Piedmontese were not having this, and put the pressure on. Eventually, on 4 July, the Venetian assembly reluctantly agreed to become part of an Italian kingdom under Charles Albert. But three weeks later came the battle of Custoza. Thereafter the Austrians besieged the city, but it held out for over a year until food shortages and a cholera epidemic compelled Manin to surrender in August 1849. In practice, Venice in 1848–9 stayed on the sidelines, as the offshore island it still was. The republic, with its promise of universal suffrage and its lack of dangerous social radicalism, retained the support of artisans and middle class alike, but it had little impact on events elsewhere, even in mainland Venetia.

Meanwhile one of the most important planks of the 'moderate' platform had collapsed. As the spiritual leader of millions of Austrian Catholics, Pius IX was horrified by Charles Albert's invasion of Austrian territory. The Pope declared that General Durando had moved legitimately to defend the Papal borders, but had exceeded his orders by crossing into Lombardy. Perhaps Durando's real offence was that he had declared the war to be 'Christian', a move calculated to alienate German-speaking Catholics from the Papacy.

On 29 April, after much agonizing, Pius went further. In a famous 'allocution', he declared that he could not declare war on, or fight against, Austria; Charles Albert was, after all, the aggressor. In retrospect this decision was inevitable. However keen Pius was on the Austrians leaving Italy, and however much he might have been prepared to turn a blind eye to 'volunteers' leaving Rome for the north, he had not envisaged war nor could he formally take sides in wartime, especially as Austria was the State that had been attacked without any provocation. Yet the speech was a huge disappointment to the patriots. The Pope's own government resigned in protest, claiming Pius had a duty to defend the Temporal Power. 'Neoguelphism' was dealt a fatal blow: clearly the Pope would not lead an Italian federation after all. Indeed, he had proclaimed that Catholics should oppose militant nationalism. All this confirmed the worst suspicions of the 'democrats' and republicans. As for the liberals and 'moderates', they had to choose: Church or State. Most of them took the secular option. So did General Durando – he put his troops at the disposal of the Piedmontese. On 29 April 1848, just a month after the Milan rising had seen priests on the barricades and the Archbishop's blessing, the Risorgimento became an anticlerical movement. It remained one thenceforth, although at local level many friars and priests remained quietly sympathetic to the 'national' cause.

THE TIME OF THE 'DEMOCRATS'

Thus by late July 1848 the 'moderate' strategy, which had relied on either the Piedmontese or the Pope, had clearly failed. The failure briefly encouraged the 'moderates'' 'democratic' rivals, still powerful in Venice and influential, after Custoza, in Tuscany and further south. In the mainland south, sporadic revolts broke out in Calabria and Basilicata, often led by students from Naples University, or by the more 'democratic' local landowners. But they were purely local, and were soon suppressed. Indeed, it is striking how soon King Ferdinand regained control of his whole kingdom, without any need for

Austrian assistance. This time the army stayed loyal. In Naples the local populace had long relied on conspicuous consumption by church and court. The Bourbons kept pasta cheap and religion respected. Press freedom and the Naples constitution remained formally in effect for a few more months, but without any significance. And by September Ferdinand controlled Sicily too.

In Tuscany the 'democrats' were quite strong in the towns. Mostly they were the usual lawyers and journalists, but they were organized in political clubs and backed by artisans and popular leaders (*capipopolo*) like the master-baker Giuseppe Dolfi in Florence and Francesco Guerrazzi in Livorno. In October urban demonstrations forced Leopold II to appoint a more 'democratic', or, at least, less aristocratic, government led by Professor Montanelli, a former 'neo-guelph' from the University of Pisa. The Tuscan 'democrats' wanted a renewed war against Austria, but not a 'princes' war' led by Charles Albert; it had to be a 'people's war', proclaimed by an Italian Constituent Assembly. The Constituent Assembly, as proposed by Montanelli, was designed to found and legitimize a new federal state. But 'neo-guelphism' was now moribund, and Cattaneo's federalist aspirations for Lombardy had also collapsed. Instead, the Constituent Assembly became the rallying-cry of more radical republicans, with a more radical significance. It came to imply a single, indivisible, unitary Italian republic, with a single constitution. This programme frightened many northern 'democrats', including Manin in Venice. It also offered little to the radical artisans in Livorno or Florence, let alone to the Catholic peasants in the countryside, who would have had to fight the 'people's war' and showed little enthusiasm at the prospect.

By early 1849 the situation in Florence had become very tense. Mass demonstrations demanded universal suffrage and support for the Roman Republic, and Montanelli's government was forced to resign. The Grand Duke decided it was time to flee. Even then the Tuscan 'democrats' did not proclaim a republic, but they did set up a provisional government, or 'Triumvirate', of three men, Montanelli, Guerrazzi and Mazzoni. The government's first act was to abolish the liberal constitution granted the previous year. It then reduced the salt tax and planted trees of liberty, but did little else. In March the Tuscans elected deputies to a legislative assembly, and to the Constituent Assembly in Rome. But then came the battle of Novara, and the game was up. By April the 'moderates' were back in power, and invited Leopold to return. Austrian troops moved in and restored the Grand Duke to his full powers, although he did not revoke the Tuscan Constitution until 1852. There was little resistance, except in Livorno.

Few Tuscans had serious grievances against their ruler, or regretted his return.

The 'democrats'' greatest success was in Rome. After Pius' 'allocution' of 29 April, a constitutional monarchy under the Pope no longer seemed a plausible long-term outcome, and a Papal-led confederation throughout Italy even less. 'Moderate' constitutionalists still ran the Papal government, but their position became weaker still after the battle of Custoza: the 'democrats' blamed the Pope, as well as Charles Albert, for the defeat. On 15 November the son of the most eminent *capopopolo*, 'Ciceruacchio' (Angelo Brunetti), had the Prime Minister, Pellegrino Rossi, assassinated. Pius, fearing the mob, fled nine days later to Neapolitan territory at Gaeta, and in February 1849 appealed to the Catholic Powers to restore the Pope's lands. The breach between Church and 'Italian' aspirations was complete. Without the Pope, the 'moderate' government in Rome was soon forced to accept 'democratic' policies like abolishing the grist-tax and, ironically, embarking on a big programme of restoring churches, in order to give employment to artisans. Meanwhile 'democrats', including both Mazzini and Garibaldi, flooded in from all over Italy and abroad. 'Democratic' clubs sprang up throughout the city and in the Legations, demanding a republic and a Constituent Assembly that would draft a new constitution, certainly for Rome and perhaps for all Italy.

In January 1849 elections were held to a Constituent Assembly (for the Papal States), by universal manhood suffrage and secret ballot. It was a triumph for the 'democrats', i.e. for lawyers and 'professionals', radical nobles, and a few *capipopolo*. On 9 February the assembly proclaimed the Roman Republic, and the end of the Temporal Power. The republic was to be a secular, egalitarian regime, enshrining popular sovereignty and autonomous local government, although governed for the time being by a triumvirate (Mazzini himself, together with Saffi and Armellini). In practice power lay with a somewhat reluctant Mazzini, who used it with surprising moderation. Church control of education and the press was abolished, as were the Inquisition, the death penalty and the government's salt and tobacco monopolies. Some Church property was seized, but in Rome itself there was little persecution of priests, and Church revenues were used to help the poorer clergy.

The Constituent Assembly produced a constitution early in July, but by then the republic was about to fall. It had always been precarious. It had very few troops, it had few friends even among the northern or Neapolitan 'democrats', and the Austrians had already triumphed in war. In France, Louis Napoleon's new government decided to forestall Austrian domination of Rome, and win Catholic support at home, by restoring the Pope. The French general Oudinot landed at Civitavecchia on 25 April and marched on Rome, as did Neapolitan troops from the south. Garibaldi performed wonders in organizing improvised defence by ex-Papal Guards and volunteers, and the republic held out for over two months. The 'myth of Garibaldi', a (true) legend of heroic devotion to duty and of glorious volunteer enthusiasm, was born. However, on 3 July 1849 French troops retook Rome, and the 'democrats' were forced to flee. Garibaldi retreated to San Marino, later to Nice and America; Mazzini returned to his London exile [69, 77, 99].

Thus the 'democrats', like the 'moderates', were defeated in 1848–9. However, they had recruited and formed over 200 volunteer corps throughout Italy, and had fought at least as well as the regular armies. In Rome, they had held out for two months, and lost to France, not Austria. They had run important states like Tuscany, Rome or Venice, for months on end. They had established a national network of friends and comrades, willing to join together again at a more propitious time. The months of the Roman Republic were Mazzini's finest hour, the only time of his life when he actually held some power, and he used it well. Thus the 'democrats'' prestige was greatly enhanced by the events of 1848–9, at least for a time. However, their problem was that they had no strategy except unending war and unending defeats. In the longer term they lost out too, more than the 'moderates'. They had, after all, gained nothing concrete. Their republics had soon been overthrown, they had no national organization with a common platform, they had no troops capable of defeating the Austrians, and they had no foreign support. The 'moderates', on the other hand, had secured a liberal constitution in Piedmont, and kept it; and Piedmont still had an army.

THE REVOLUTION THAT FAILED

Historians have often remarked how 'local' – municipal, rather than regional, let alone 'national' – the various revolts of 1848 were, and how much they differed among themselves. True, most insurgents in northern Italy wanted rid of the Austrians, but they had little else in common. In Venice, the 'democrats' proclaimed the Venetian Republic, harking back fifty years; and the *terraferma* remained noticeably aloof. In Sicily and the deep mainland south, both 'liberals' and 'people' rose against Naples, not against Austria, and certainly not for 'Italy'. Even 'democrats' in Sicily, Venice and Naples showed little sympathy for the troubles of the Roman Republic. Many Sicilian 'moderates' from other cities welcomed Ferdinand back in September 1848, having disliked rule from Palermo even more than rule from Naples. In Tuscany, Guerrazzi's insurrection in February 1849 aimed at an independent Tuscan Republic. In the Papal States, Bologna was revolutionary but most of the rest of Emilia-Romagna was not; and the insurgents of late 1848 wanted an end to Papal rule and the founding of a 'democratic' Roman Republic, far more clearly than they wanted anything else. They murdered Pellegrino Rossi, a tough-minded reformer, in order to bring it about. In Piedmont, there was no revolt, just the traditional Savoyard expansionism, mitigated by a liberal-sounding constitution forced on a reluctant king. True, in Lombardy and Tuscany insurrectionary leaders 'volunteered' the union of their states with their neighbours, but the Lombards had little choice, and the Tuscans deliberately chose republican Rome rather than monarchist Piedmont.

The most serious effort to create a 'national' movement was the Customs League of November 1847, but even this was agreed only by Piedmont, Tuscany and the Papal States, and it had no political powers. Efforts to give it some in 1848 soon foundered: Charles Albert wanted war, the Pope did not. Apart from that, one can point to the 'united war effort' of Piedmont, Tuscany, Naples and the Papal States in spring 1848 against the Austrians, but this lasted only a few weeks and ended in acrimony long before the battle of Custoza. One might also, at a pinch, see Montanelli's proposals for a 'Constituent Assembly' as a serious attempt at (federal) unity, but it received very little support outside Tuscany and the Papal States. Perhaps the only people in 1848 who really wanted a united Italy were the Genoese and the Sardinians, both of whom wanted it in order to diminish Piedmontese control of their territory.

The 1848 revolts showed, yet again, that the existing regimes were vulnerable. Neither their armies nor their police were any use against barricades, nor against mass demonstrations by rioting artisans, organised by popular leaders (*capipopolo*). Unarmed craftsmen rose in Palermo, Milan, Venice, Livorno, Florence, Bologna, Rome and many other cities. They secured new governments and constitutions. They even drove Radetzky's 12,000 troops out of Milan. They were a real threat, feared not only by governments but also by the 'moderates' and by many 'democrats' – although the so-called 'dangerous classes', of vagrants and sub-proletarian urban poor, turned out to be docile after all. Only in Naples could the king rely, more or less, on the urban populace, and even there the new liberal doctrines of free trade were exposing artisans to very unwelcome competition. In the countryside, unrest was more manageable. True, the Lombard peasants rose against the Austrians in spring 1848, and some peasants were also active in Sicily and the mainland south. But they were usually inspired by purely local issues – land ownership, grazing rights and so forth. The peasants had limited horizons. They wanted land near their own villages, not a united Italy, and they well knew that neither 'moderates' nor 'democrats' would give it them.

The real leaders of the revolts were the educated nobles and professional men, particularly lawyers and journalists. These were the ones who were most interested in political schemes and in drafting constitutions, who wrote in the hundreds of new journals and were elected to the new assemblies, who founded the political clubs of Tuscany and Rome, and who held top posts in the new governments. They were the men who debated political issues; they were the voice of 'public opinion'. They were active both as 'moderates' and 'democrats'. Indeed, apart from the fact that the *capipopolo* and artisans were predominantly 'democrat', there was not much difference socially between 'moderates' and 'democrats', although 'democrats' tended to be younger, more anticlerical and more southern. Despite the artisan revolts and the universal manhood suffrage, it is striking how political debate remained – or perhaps became – an elite activity, confined to the educated. In the 'democratic' clubs of Florence, anyone could join, but only the educated were allowed to speak. The free press, in fact, made intellectuals far more significant than before. Students – the intellectuals and professional men of the future – were also prominent in 1848. Most of the major university cities had insurrections; university teachers like Montanelli and Saffi were leading activists [111 *p. 166*].

However, the events of 1848–49 also showed that mainland Italy was not as insurrectionary as all that. Early in 1848 most rulers granted constitutions peacefully. The insurrections in Milan and Venice occurred only because Metternich had fallen in Vienna and because the Austrian empire appeared to be crumbling. They were led by 'a backward-looking aristocracy, with an absolute king and a Pope', as Cattaneo later complained [27 *p. 19*]. The Mazzinian notion of a 'people's war' proved unrealistic, since the peasants had never heard of 'Italy' and were hostile mainly to the local landowners. True, volunteer troops were at least as effective as mercenaries or conscripts, but they did not defeat the Austrians or the French.

If 'the people' could not drive the Austrians out, nor could the princes, at least by themselves. Austria, after all, won the war against Piedmont not once but twice. A major lesson of 1848–9 was that Italy could not, in fact, 'go it alone', and would not be allowed to. The only way to expel the Austrians was to secure French help [*Doc. 6*]; and even that would not bring about unification. Insurrection in Milan meant war with Austria; and insurrection in Rome meant invasion by France. So both these Powers, and perhaps others, would have to be defeated, or squared, before any unification was possible. Unification could only occur as part of a general European settlement, acceptable to the Powers. And this did not look likely.

Another important lesson of the 1848–9 risings was that Pius IX would not lead, or even support, any 'national' movement against foreign rule. Worse, he had appealed successfully to foreign Powers to restore him to his Temporal Power. Gioberti and the 'neo-guelphs' had been proved wrong, and liberal Catholicism was discredited. Henceforth 'national' sympathizers had to be willing to fight the Vatican, if not the Church as a whole. The Pope's Temporal Power was now under attack from 'patriots', as it had not been before 1848. Only once it had vanished, they argued, could Rome assume her rightful status as capital of the new, secular 'Italy'. And if the Pope was not willing to lead the patriotic movement, who was? There could be only one answer to that question: Piedmont.

THE NEW RESTORATION

After August 1849 the former rulers (except Ferdinand of Austria, Charles Albert of Piedmont and Charles II of Parma, who had all abdicated) were back in control of their states. It was a 'second Restoration', considerably more repressive than the first. Italy was still ruled by 'foreigners', but more openly than before. There were French troops in Rome; the Austrians kept garrisons in Tuscany (until 1855), Parma, Modena and even the Papal States, as well as in Lombardy-Venetia. Lombardy remained under military rule until 1857. Except in Piedmont, the constitutions of 1848 were soon rescinded. Press censorship resumed and officialdom ruled once more, with few concessions to 'enlightened' public opinion. The discontented had far less hope of imminent radical change than in the heady days of 1846–7, but they also had a greater sense of what was possible. Expectations had been aroused, but not satisfied. And the discontented were now more numerous. Many people had been compromised in 1848–9, and were forced into exile in Piedmont, Switzerland or France. This was true not just of the 'democratic' revolutionaries, but of many respectable 'moderate' landowners, particularly in Lombardy [110].

Indeed, in Lombardy the Austrians proceeded to lose their previous reputation for efficiency and impartial administration, and acquired one for vindictive tyranny instead. Radetzky rightly assumed the Lombard nobles and professional classes hated him, and responded in kind. Prominent ex-members or supporters of the provisional government were heavily fined. The estates of exiles were sequestered, as were 20,000 more estates after an abortive rising in Milan in 1853. Nobles' town houses in Milan were requisitioned for Austrian troops, and very high taxes were imposed on landowners. Thus the Austrians persecuted the rich and wooed – unsuccessfully – the one group they thought reliable, the peasantry, for example by abolishing the poll tax. Radetzky's revenge may have been commendably egalitarian, but it was bad politics, and terrible public relations. It alienated the most influential families – the Casati, the Borromeo, the Pallavicino, the Belgioioso – making them even more likely to throw in their lot with the property-respecting Piedmontese. The Piedmontese government thoughtfully encouraged this process, by making 400,000 lire available to dispossessed exiles living in Piedmont. And, of course, many Milanese artisans and merchants depended on the nobles' custom. Admittedly conditions improved markedly after 1857, when Archduke Maximilian became viceroy, but by then the damage had been done [*Doc. 8*].

In Rome, on the other hand, the aristocracy was delighted at Pius IX's return, although many of the middle and lower classes were not. The Pope's real problems were financial. The government could not afford to build proper defences for the city, despite the evident lessons of 1849. It could not even cover ordinary expenditure without borrowing money from the Rothschilds in Paris; conditions for the Jews improved markedly as a result. Pius did rebuild a Papal army of 8,000 mercenaries, but the task of defending Rome and the Temporal Power had now fallen to the French.

Elsewhere life was not so different from before 1848. In Tuscany, the Grand Duke continued his previous policy of moderate reform and useful public works, especially railways. The country was stable and landowners contented, although they needed greater export opportunities for their wine. In Naples, too, the liberals were quiescent. Southern 'democrats' continued to press for a constitution, but without much conviction. The Mazzinians continued to see the south as the fulcrum of the Italian revolution, a view that had little justification but did much to colour how northerners saw southern society, then and later. Gladstone's famous phrase about Naples in April 1851, 'the negation of God, erected into a system of government', owed much to Mazzinian propaganda [48 *p. xiv*; 50; 87, i, *pp. 292* ff.].

Yet if the various regimes were less attractive in the 1850s, so too was the 'democratic' option. Property-owners had had a nasty shock in 1848–9. Thereafter they wanted security, order and adequate policing, not insurrections or democracy. Outside Lombardy, most governments were distrusted not because they were oppressive but because they had been ineffective and unable to guarantee public order. The old regimes had survived but were clearly still vulnerable, and too dependent on a weakened Austria. The lesson was not lost on conservative army officers, officials and landowners. There might not be much future in staying loyal. They began to look north-westwards, to Piedmont. The 'liberal' Constitution, still in force there, did not seem too bad, and was certainly a better prospect than rule by demagogic radicals. Piedmont had little disorder, and her aristocrats were firmly in charge. Moreover, she had an army and a rural police force, the *carabinieri*, that might preserve landowners' interests. So office-holders, particularly in Lombardy and Tuscany, began hedging their bets. After 1848 the 'Historic Right' was born, an alliance of royalist bureaucrats and property-owning liberals throughout Italy. It aimed at combining the old tough policing and the new civil liberties, the old royal prerogatives and the new parliamentary scrutiny.

CONSTITUTIONAL PIEDMONT

Only in Piedmont did the 1848 Constitution survive (see page 51), confirmed by the new King Victor Emanuel II on his accession. This proved vitally important. Indeed, arguably Italy was unified eleven years later only because the 1848–9 revolutions failed to produce a series of constitutional monarchies in Italy. They produced only one, which thus had greatness thrust upon it. The Piedmontese *Statuto* meant that Italians did not have to choose between 'nationalism' and 'liberalism'. They might go together, but only in Piedmont.

Thousands of exiles – estimates vary from 20,000 to 100,000 at different times – flocked to Piedmont and Liguria from all over Italy, many aided by the government if need be (although there were also plenty of exiles *from* Piedmont or Liguria too, including Mazzini himself in London). These refugees made a huge difference. They sought refuge, but they also founded journals that could be published freely (or fairly freely, for the government could and did seize journals on public order grounds), debated public issues and created a lively 'Italian' political culture. Some became deputies in the Piedmontese parliament, or even government ministers. They helped transform remote, provincial Turin, with its French-speaking court, its still harsh penal laws and its undistinguished university, into the improbable centre of Italian cultural and political liberalism.

The new Constitution was fairly open-ended: it could be interpreted in more 'liberal' ways as time went on. Even at the start it forced 'moderate' Piedmontese politicians to behave in strange new ways: to fight elections, to learn parliamentary procedures and to win at least some degree of popular support. Although court and crown retained a great deal of influence, the successful politician henceforth would be the one who could manipulate parliament and press. Above all, the Constitution gave Piedmont the approval of foreign Powers. Piedmont, previously as absolutist a state as any other in Italy, and one that had insisted on complete 'fusion' with Lombardy and Venetia in 1848 even in mid-war, suddenly became politically correct. She might have lost the war (twice), but she had gained an unlikely new status, both liberal haven and national paladin.

The outstanding achievement of the post-1848 governments in Piedmont, particularly that led by Massimo d'Azeglio between 1849 and 1852, was to make the new parliamentary system work. This was not a simple matter. In 1849 a 'democrat'-dominated Chamber of Deputies refused to ratify the peace treaty with Austria. D'Azeglio had to dissolve parliament and then, fearing defeat at the elections, he persuaded the king to proclaim that the future of constitutional government rested on the deputies being 'responsible'. This 'proclamation of Moncalieri' was crude electoral blackmail: electors were told to vote for the right deputies, or risk losing Constitution and parliament altogether. The Minister of the Interior contributed too, by urging public officials to vote correctly, and threatening them with dismissal if they did not. The electors did the royal bidding, the peace treaty was ratified, and d'Azeglio's liberal government kept a reasonably secure majority for the next three years. But it was hardly a good start for the new parliamentary regime, nor was it a tactic that could be repeated.

The problem was that governments needed the support of the deputies in key votes, but deputies were independent-minded. They were elected in single-member constituencies in which 250 people, on average, actually voted. In many constituencies the number was much smaller, and the candidate backed by the local 'notable' – prominent landowner or lawyer – was virtually certain to be re-elected however he behaved or voted. Organized parties did not exist, just groups of like-minded friends or vague labels like 'Right' and 'Left'. 'Right' deputies, of whom there were over twenty in number in 1853, were clerical, strong in Savoy, suspicious of free trade and liberal reforms, and convinced it would all end in revolution. The 'Left', with around 50 deputies, was more 'democratic' in sympathy, distrusted aristocrats like Cavour and was strong in Liguria. But neither group was disciplined, and plenty of deputies voted as they pleased on each issue. Balbo himself, one of Cavour's closest colleagues, opposed the government's anti-Church laws. In these circumstances governments had no option but to bring dissident groups 'into the system', by means of concessions on policy and appointments. In short, they had to be bought off.

Although d'Azeglio remained Prime Minister until late 1852, Piedmontese politics became increasingly dominated by one man, Camillo Benso di Cavour. Cavour entered public life only in late 1847, when press restrictions were lifted. With Cesare Balbo, he founded and edited the *Risorgimento*, which soon became a highly influential liberal periodical. Early in 1848 it urged the king to grant a liberal Constitution, and took some of the credit when Charles Albert did so. Within a few weeks Balbo had become the first 'constitutional' Prime Minister of Piedmont, and Cavour himself entered parliament in June 1848. He soon made his mark. He had studied parliamentary procedure in other countries, a topic unknown to practically all his colleagues. He had travelled widely in France and Britain, although not in Italy itself, and had studied these advanced economies very closely. Indeed, he had many international contacts among bankers and businessmen, and knew far more about European business and finance than any other Piedmontese politician. Strong-minded, able and aristocratic, he had a strong gambling streak and was involved in several speculative ventures, including railway-building. He was sociable, self-confident and amusing; he was also a shrewd judge of character, and distinctly flexible, not to say opportunist, in his political manoeuvres. Above all, he was a practical man. He had no time for the levelling rhetoric of the Mazzinians, and had detested the stuffy obscurantism of Charles Albert's regime. He had run his own family estates, and he was determined to open up the isolated and protected Piedmontese economy to the outside world [62, 76, 105].

In 1850 Cavour became Minister of Agriculture and Commerce, and the next year Minister of Finance. He signed commercial treaties with all Piedmont's major trading partners, including Austria and the *Zollverein*, thus reducing tariffs. Within ten years trade – especially in textiles, silk, wine and rice – had trebled, so tax revenues actually increased. He halved the cost of postage, and again postal revenue soon increased. But Cavour was no simple-minded free-market liberal. He reduced tariffs, but he also sharply raised direct taxes, for instance on land, and he firmly believed in state intervention. Like Charles Albert, he subsidized banks, railways, and shipping lines; and he was quite happy to spend public money on major improvements, like Alpine tunnels or irrigation schemes. By 1859 Piedmont and Liguria had 850 km of railway, almost half that in all Italy. New companies sprang up, mostly dependent on state orders. Foreign – especially French – investment flowed in. However, not every commercial speculation succeeded, and budget deficits rose alarmingly. Cavour did not greatly care. He knew what railways might achieve, and he was bent on 'modernization from above'. Money could always be borrowed, if need be from London to avoid excessive dependence on Paris; liberal institutions would always provide legitimacy. His policies were remarkably successful, though they left a crippling public debt to his successors (725 million lire in 1859, compared with 120 million in 1847). Piedmont acquired a rather exaggerated image of progress and modernity, and Cavour's reputation grew.

Early in 1852 Cavour, still Minister of Finance in d'Azeglio's cabinet, made a famous deal with the leader of the parliamentary 'Left' liberals, Urbano Rattazzi. Their 'marriage' (*connubio*) gave the government the votes of the Left, and overall in 1853 about 130 deputies out of 204. It kept the clericals and conservatives out of influence, and it rendered the Mazzinians innocuous – they could hardly revolt against a freely-elected 'Left-wing' government. The *connubio*, in short, gave Cavour an essential parliamentary cover. He became Prime Minister in November 1852, with Rattazzi as Speaker of the Chamber (later Minister of the Interior), and for a few key years his position was assured. Not for ever, of course. Cavour had to continue to suppress the republican press and bribe the other newspapers, and to practise the black arts of parliamentary management. Even then he lost the 1857 elections.

The basis of the *connubio* was anticlericalism. The Church was fair game. After 1848 she was generally seen as a pro-Austrian obstacle to Italian unification. Her wealth and lands, especially those of the contemplative religious orders of monks, were tempting plunder to secular politicians bent on expensive public works. The d'Azeglio government had already adopted much of the Left's Church policy, by abolishing the clergy's civil jurisdiction and right of asylum, and by reducing the number of Church holidays to six a year. It also introduced a bill on civil marriage, although in order to placate the king Cavour abandoned this during his 1852 manoeuvres to replace d'Azeglio as Prime Minister. The Cavour government went further. It proposed to end the Church's virtual monopoly of education, and to suppress the monastic orders. Again, Cavour had to contend with pressure from Rome and with the king's intermittently tender conscience, which between them saved nearly half the monasteries. In 1857, after years of wrangling over Church-state relations, came retribution. 'Clerical' candidates did well at the polls: around 80 deputies, a third of the total, were reckoned to be clerical sympathizers, although twenty of them were excluded from parliament because of alleged 'pressure from the pulpit' on the voters. Even so, the government lost over 40 seats, and its majority disappeared. Cavour hastily dropped Rattazzi and formed a more conservative government without Left-wing support. He himself became Minister of the Interior, as well as retaining the other key posts. The elections thus resulted in little change. Representative institutions in Italy clearly had their limitations. They were useful when they bolstered executive power; they were ignored when they did not [*75 p. 70*].

The anticlerical laws confirmed the 1848 breach between Church and 'national' aspirations. They had one further consequence. They were manifestly a state confiscation of private property, and as such horrified some of the senior judges. The judiciary had therefore to be purged and brought firmly under government control. Soon all judges were appointed, transferred and promoted by the Minister of Justice. The same regime was imposed on the senior civil servants. Cavour thus created a more centralized administrative and judicial machinery, forced to obey government orders. Even so, his reliable, committed supporters were few. Those few tended, therefore, to be given key posts across a wide range of the public sector, flitting easily from senior civil servant to judge, from parliamentary deputy to chief of police, or acting as Prefect supervising local government and public administration.

Even then Cavour tried to run everything himself. He used parliament to conceal, or to legitimate, his own quasi-personal rule. In practice, only the king could obstruct him, and only then on 'issues of conscience' like civil marriage, or sometimes on military or foreign policy matters where the royal prerogative was accepted if ill-defined. However, Cavour's 'top-down' modernizing reforms ran into difficulties in the late 1850s, as parliament became less manageable and state finances ran dry. Moreover, by that time Cavour needed to conciliate the French Emperor Napoleon III, who disapproved of too much domestic liberty and who was protector of the Church.

However, Cavour's greatest domestic political achievement lay outside parliament. By the mid-1850s he was drawing into his orbit some of the radical 'democrats' and erstwhile republicans, and outflanking the others. This was unexpected, and had unexpected consequences later on. Yet the explanation is simple. The Mazzinians' revolutionary strategy became ever less plausible as time went on. The 'democrats' had high prestige in 1849 and continued to plot, but achieved nothing. In February 1853 a rising in Milan was soon put down, with 50 executions; there were futile risings in Lunigiana; in 1857 Carlo Pisacane seized a Piedmontese merchant ship, freed 300 political prisoners on the island of Ponza, and sailed on to Sapri in Calabria, hoping to instigate a peasant revolt. The peasants, yet again, showed no interest. Moreover, the 'democrats' constantly quarrelled among themselves, particularly in their rival accounts of why the 1848–9 revolutions had failed. Mazzini's insistence on Italian 'unity', i.e. a unitary, centralized state, was not shared by many other 'democrats' and republicans: Cattaneo, Ferrari, Manin and Montanelli were all federalists, and Asproni soon became one. Mazzini's social proposals were not popular either; and his other main argument, that Italians should rule themselves, had now become a commonplace which people no longer needed to learn from the Master.

The 'democrats' in the 1830s and 1840s had been few, and those few mostly in secret societies. After 1848 there were thousands of them, mostly in exile – penniless, friendless and jobless. Their wives and children were left behind, persecuted and neglected. The exiles congregated in Turin, Genoa, Paris or London, and reflected on their glory days in 1848–9. Many of them came to realize that the 'Italian People' was not revolutionary after all, and that the old regimes were not necessarily on the verge of collapse. They also soon learned that even exile politics was dominated by the 'moderates', mostly richer men with connections who might find you a job or lodging. No wonder that some of the 'democrats' were tempted to break ranks. Anticlerical Piedmont, under Cavour, did not seem so bad after all. It might have a king but it also had an army, and it clearly wanted to drive out the Austrians. Perhaps, after all, it might be possible to be both patriotic and monarchical [Doc. 9]?

In 1855–6 a group of prominent 'democrat' exiles in Turin, led by the Lombard aristocrat Giorgio Pallavicino and later by the Sicilian journalist Giuseppe La Farina, formed the Italian National Society, pledged to the cause of Italian independence, but also to support Piedmont and Victor Emanuel in that cause. It offered the 'democrats' a more plausible strategy, and also some chance of official favour. Initially the best-known convert, who brought over many supporters, was Daniele Manin, but soon the Society secured an even more influential supporter, Giuseppe Garibaldi. The Society was not large (it never had more than 2,000 members at any one time) but it was full of writers and journalists keeping anti-Austrian sentiment alive. Its journal, the *Piccolo Corriere d'Italia*, portrayed every region of Italy as yearning improbably for liberation: portraits of Victor Emanuel were selling well in Milan, and the girls of Piacenza would not marry anyone who had not fought for independence [54 p. 122]. Thus was 'public opinion' created, and made into a political force.

Above all, the Society had a direct political role. It aimed to stir up revolt all over Italy, while allowing the Piedmontese government to disclaim any responsibility. It was, therefore, a marvellous instrument in the hands of an ambitious and unscrupulous politician like Cavour. The Society was most effective in Romagna and the Papal States, with their numerous minor noblemen and their tradition of clandestine organization. Elsewhere, however, it was often simply a propaganda body; committed to direct action in theory, but with little appeal to 'democrat' activists in practice. Few Lombard, Tuscan or southern 'democrats' joined it. In fact, it often had more appeal to 'moderates', as a relatively safe way of establishing some 'national' credentials in an uncertain future, while being meantime a useful network of friendships and personal links among the 'great and the good' [54].

CAVOUR AND FOREIGN POLICY

Cavour's domestic achievements were insignificant compared to his diplomatic triumphs. For him, the lesson of 1848–9 was clear: Italy could not 'go it alone'. Indeed, Italy could probably not be united at all, but there might be a chance of Piedmont annexing Lombardy and Venetia once again. Even for that she would need allies. That meant France, ruled by Louis Napoleon until December 1851 as President, thereafter as Emperor Napoleon III. Napoleon believed in his own Napoleonic legend, and wanted to make his mark on Europe. As a young man in 1831 he had even taken part in a *Carbonaro* rising in Romagna, and he sometimes saw himself as liberator of the peoples from alien rule. He was anxious to weaken Austria in northern Italy. But he would not support any dangerous 'democratic' or republican movement; order and discipline would have to be maintained. Furthermore, he was pledged to protect the Temporal Power, and he kept French troops in Rome.

Cavour's task, therefore, was to conciliate Napoleon III and seek a military alliance with him, directed against Austria, while playing down Italian 'national' aspirations inasmuch as they affected Rome. As for southern Italy, Cavour did not want it nor could he contemplate acquiring it, for there was a 'Bonapartist' pretender to the throne of Naples, the French Emperor's cousin Lucien Murat. However, Cavour's strategy was not easy. Napoleon III could hardly be expected to make war on Austria simply to aggrandize Piedmont. France would need a reward. True, Napoleon would be pleased if the ultimate outcome were a weak Italian federation, headed nominally by the Pope although in practice by Piedmont: such a federation would owe a huge debt of gratitude to France, and be a virtual client-state. He would be even more pleased if Lucien Murat could be installed on the throne of the Two Sicilies. But even this might not be enough. The obvious reward for France was Savoy, the ancestral home of the Piedmontese royal House and still ruled by the Piedmontese monarchs, as was the (large) county of Nice. Would Napoleon III insist on acquiring Savoy, in return for helping Victor Emanuel II to acquire Lombardy? If so, would Victor Emanuel be willing to give up the land of his fathers?

Cavour also had to consider the interests of the other Powers. The Prussians were keen to see Austria weakened for their own reasons in Germany, but they did not want French power increased. The British, impressed by Cavour's liberalism and by his commitment to free trade, would also have preferred to see Austria out of Italy, but similarly feared greater French influence in the Mediterranean. Both these Powers were Protestant, approved of Piedmont's anticlerical legislation and had no particular wish to maintain the Pope's Temporal Power. In general, most European countries had signed favourable commercial treaties with Piedmont in 1850–51, and all respectable European opinion was outraged in 1853 when the Austrians seized the Lombard exiles' property.

In 1854 came Cavour's great opportunity. The French and British became involved in the Crimean War against Russia. Soon their soldiers were destroyed by cholera, and they needed Piedmontese (and, for that matter, Austrian) support. Victor Emanuel II, thirsting for military glory, was anxious to join in. Cavour, initially, was not: the war would bring no obvious benefits, and few Piedmontese wished to get involved, least of all if Austria were on the same side. But when Cavour discovered that the king was planning to dismiss him and appoint a more warlike prime minister, and furthermore had already begun discussing terms with France, and that Austria might join in too, he realised he had no choice. He had to join the war, to keep his job; and he could not allow the French to be beholden only to the Austrians. Cavour bullied his cabinet into agreeing, and in March 1855 Piedmont declared war on Russia. She sent 18,000 troops to the Crimea; nearly 2,000 of them died of cholera. Even so, the war turned out to be surprisingly successful. In August the Piedmontese were prominent in the victory at Chernaya Rechka, which brought about the surrender of Sebastopol. In December the Austrians finally threatened to enter the war at last, and the Russians hastily sued for peace.

Cavour attended the subsequent Paris peace conference as a victor, but the Austrians counted as victors too, and the British and French were unwilling to alienate her. Cavour therefore acted the responsible European statesman, always a role he enjoyed and one which never failed to impress the British. He sought no gains for Piedmont, but he did manage to secure a debate on Italy, in which he urged that the other Italian states should follow Piedmont's wise example and implement liberal reforms, as the best way of preventing revolution. This was, of course, an implicit attack on Austria, the Papal States and the Two Sicilies, but Cavour went no further. The conference concluded in a warm glow of self-congratulatory platitudes, and Cavour went home, apparently empty-handed.

The real situation was worse than he thought. He soon discovered, to his fury, that Britain, France and Austria had signed a secret treaty designed to contain Russia. Even so, Cavour had achieved much. Piedmont, almost for the first time, had taken her place – a minor place, admittedly, but a place – among the Powers at a major European peace conference. He had ensured that the 'Italian question' was recognised as existing, and that it was discussed by the Powers. By stressing Piedmont's progressive reforms, he had impressed European opinion and outflanked all Italian rivals – indeed, France and Britain broke off diplomatic relations with the Two Sicilies shortly afterwards, on the grounds that it was a tyranny. Above all, the Crimean War had shattered the Vienna settlement of 1815. For forty years the European balance of power had rested on Russo-Austrian friendship. But now those two continental Powers had almost fought each other, and would clearly remain rivals in south-east Europe (and did so until 1918). Equally clearly, Napoleon III would be anxious now for more glory and more territory, and he owed a debt to Piedmont. In short, the Crimean War created an entirely new diplomatic situation, which both Napoleon III and Cavour might seek to exploit [*Doc. 10*].

In the event, matters were precipitated by an Italian republican exile in Paris, Felice Orsini. In January 1858 he threw a bomb at Napoleon III, missing the Emperor but killing eight others. Condemned to death, he wrote from prison to Napoleon explaining that it was the miserable state of Italy that had made his act necessary: a French republic would withdraw troops from Rome, and would help the fight against Austria. On the eve of execution, he appealed to the Emperor to help the Italian cause, or risk future assassination attempts. Shaken, Napoleon pressed Cavour to clamp down on the Mazzinians. Cavour obliged, closing down their leading journals and ending jury trials in cases of libel. But both men realised this was not a long-term solution. Perhaps Orsini had been right: Napoleon III might have to act, to prevent trouble in future. In any case, both he and Cavour wanted war against Austria anyway, so why wait?

Cavour sent a private emissary, Costantino Nigra, to Paris, and secret negotiations soon began. In July 1858 Cavour himself was invited to visit the Emperor secretly at Plombières, in the Vosges. They agreed to fight the Austrians, if a suitable pretext could be found: Austria would have to be provoked into declaring the war herself. If all went well in the war, the Austrians would be driven out of Italy. Piedmont would receive both Lombardy and Venetia, the two small duchies of Modena and Parma, and also Emilia-Romagna and the Legations. She would thus form a new Kingdom of Upper Italy. But there was no intention of uniting the whole peninsula. Tuscany would remain independent, indeed would swallow up Umbria and the Marches from the Papal States and become a Kingdom of Central Italy. Rome and Latium would remain in Papal hands, and the Kingdom of the Two Sicilies would continue in the South. An Italian confederation would be set up, with the Pope as President. France, as a reward for her efforts, would receive Savoy (Nice was added later, in the formal second treaty between the two countries in January 1859).

Napoleon III no doubt hoped to see Lucien Murat on the throne of Naples and a French *protégé* installed in Florence, but such aspirations were not included in the formal agreement. But it did include, as a guarantee that the agreement would be kept, provision that Victor Emanuel's fifteen-year-old daughter, Princess Maria Clotilde, would marry Napoleon III's middle-aged cousin Jerome. Thus a prominent Bonaparte would marry into one of the oldest royal houses in Europe. One concession was made to progressive values. The peoples of the various states were to be asked, at a plebiscite, who should rule them. Even so, it was clear that Victor Emanuel II would secure a far larger kingdom; that Napoleon III would acquire Savoy and at least one client-state; and that both rulers would enjoy the prestige of a glorious war. And no other Power would intervene to spoil the fun: Austria was diplomatically isolated [*Doc. 11*].

With this agreement in his pocket, Cavour spent the winter of 1858–9 preparing for war and trying to provoke the Austrians into declaring it. The army was mobilized, the reserves were called up, and the National Society encouraged to recruit volunteers. Nearly 20,000 volunteers did come to Turin, mostly from exile or central Italy. Garibaldi was appointed commander of the Alpine Hunters' regiment. It was obvious to all that Piedmont wanted war, but provoking the Austrians proved tricky. The National Society was asked to organize an insurrection in Massa-Carrara, within the Duchy of Modena, so that the Austrians would invade and provide a *casus belli*. This plan misfired since hardly anybody joined the insurrection – rather to Cavour's relief, as he had feared it might succeed only too well and trigger a real revolution.

Cavour needed to demonstrate to foreign opinion that all Italy was groaning under a tyrannical yoke and desperately awaiting liberation, but nobody really believed this except the Mazzinians, who had a quite different liberation in mind. And the only way of demonstrating that mass discontent really existed was by insurrection, which might get out of hand. Napoleon III suggested, and Victor Emanuel agreed, that in the king's speech at the opening of parliament he should speak of a 'cry of anguish' (*grido di dolore*) coming from all Italy, but even this implausible and very public claim failed to provoke the Austrians [*Doc. 12*].

Meanwhile the other Powers, anxious to prevent war, were organizing a conference to settle the Franco-Austrian dispute peacefully, and Napoleon III himself was having second thoughts. For a time Cavour's war schemes seemed lost, and he even seems to have contemplated suicide. An international conference was no use to Cavour. Even if it gave Lombardy to Piedmont, the Austrians might easily start a war a few years later and win it back; and how could he contain the 'democrats', or justify giving up Savoy? Eventually the Austrians rescued him. For no obvious reason except that they could not afford to stay mobilized themselves, they finally reacted and demanded that Piedmont demobilize her troops. On Piedmont's refusal, Austria declared war. Cavour's gamble had begun to come off [*Doc. 13*].

It is worth comparing these diplomatic manoeuvres with the events of 1848–9. In 1848 genuine insurrections and popular enthusiasm triggered the war against Austria, a war fought by Italians and often inspired by national rhetoric as well as by a demand for liberty and constitutionalism. In 1858–9, on the other hand, the whole process was 'top-down'. War was planned a year ahead, deliberately and secretly, by a tiny handful of French and Piedmontese politicians who often deplored the lack of plausible popular unrest. These men had no interest in Italian unity and were not motivated by zeal for constitutional liberties. They were, however, very keen on acquiring territory for themselves and on furthering their dynastic ambitions, as the fate of Maria Clotilde showed. Furthermore, the war of 1859 might easily have been – indeed, almost was – prevented by the other Powers; it occurred only because the Austrians miscalculated. In any case, it was at least as much a French initiative as it was Italian. It was Napoleon III who invited Cavour to Plombières, who provided the bulk of the troops when war began, and who expected the real benefits.

8 THE UNIFICATION OF ITALY, 1859–61

After 1848 Cavour had concluded that only the French could defeat
Austria. The campaign of summer 1859 proved his point. Two hundred thousand French troops, brought to Italy rapidly by rail,
commanded by Napoleon III personally, and using the new rifled
field artillery, invaded Lombardy and won the battle of Magenta on
4 June. Four days later Victor Emanuel and Napoleon III entered
Milan in triumph. Three weeks later the French won another victory
at Solferino, north-west of Mantua, on this occasion with the help of
Piedmontese troops at the nearby battle of San Martino, and perhaps
even more from the Italian soldiers in the Austrian army, who
deserted *en masse*. These were massive, hard-fought battles, with
more casualties than in any war since the days of Napoleon I: 40,000
were killed at Solferino alone, quite apart from those who died of
typhus.

The Piedmontese army, with its 60,000 troops, performed hardly
better than in 1848–9, and the large number of volunteers – 20,000
initially, more later – were often distrusted. Predominantly artisans or
students from the centre-north, most of these volunteers were, or had
been, 'democrats' or republicans; but now they were in the king's
army, fighting for the king's cause. They proved that there was some
popular support for the 'national' programme, and they were useful
in the fighting. Italy might not be able to 'go it alone', but she could
make a contribution. Moreover, Garibaldi's 3000 Alpine Hunters
(*Cacciatori delle Alpi*), mostly volunteers fighting as a virtually autonomous unit, were highly successful and won Como and Varese by
23 May, before the battle of Magenta. Even so, it was noticeable that
the local inhabitants, either in the towns or the countryside, showed
little interest and gave little support.

Even after Solferino the Austrians were not really defeated. They
still held the Quadrilateral fortresses, to say nothing of all Venetia
and parts of Lombardy. They had 150,000 men, and were receiving

reinforcements and supplies over the Brenner. They could hold out for months if need be, and the Piedmontese had few siege weapons, despite their pre-war promises to the French. Napoleon III began to have second thoughts. He had been horrified by the carnage at Solferino, and he could not face the further battles that would be needed to take the fortresses. How many more French soldiers could he sacrifice on the Lombard plains, without a revolt at home? Piedmont was clearly an unreliable ally, both militarily and politically, and was playing her own game in the duchies and in Papal Romagna (see below). There was therefore a nasty possibility of Catholic France being dragged into a war against the Pope. Then there was the financial cost. Piedmont had promised to pay all the costs of the war, but by the end of June that already came to at least 350 million francs, and the French Emperor knew that Piedmont would never manage to pay up. Above all, Prussia was making ominous diplomatic moves, and was mobilizing troops on the Rhine. Napoleon III had become dangerously isolated.

He therefore began negotiations directly with the Austrian Emperor Francis Joseph, who was also in Italy commanding the Austrian troops. On 8 July an armistice was signed, and three days later the two emperors reached agreement at Villafranca. Most of Lombardy, by this time in French hands, would be handed over to the Piedmontese. Austria would retain Venetia, and also Mantua and Peschiera. The central Italian duchies would remain under their existing rulers, as would Savoy and Nice. An Italian confederation, including Austria because of Venetia, would be set up under the Pope. The Plombières agreement was forgotten. Cavour was not consulted. Victor Emanuel was asked to sign up to the new arrangements. He had little choice: Piedmont could not fight on her own. So he agreed. Again, Cavour was not consulted. Furious at Napoleon III's betrayal and Victor Emanuel's compliance, Cavour promptly resigned. General Alfonso La Marmora became Prime Minister. The war of 1859 was over. Lombardy alone, or most of it, had been gained. In November the Treaty of Zurich confirmed the main lines of the Villafranca settlement. A European conference was to be called, to organize the Italian confederation and to resolve the fate of the central Italian duchies.

CENTRAL ITALY

But the fate of the central Italian duchies had already been decided. The first Austrian defeat at Magenta meant that the Austrians had to withdraw their troops from the duchies and the Legations. On 14

June the Duchess-Regent of Parma and the Duke of Modena both fled their duchies, in the by now traditional manner. Piedmontese troops moved in, as agreed at Plombières. In the Legations of Emilia-Romagna local 'popular revolts', in fact usually carefully orchestrated by members of the Italian National Society, overthrew the established administrations. As in 1848, the leading aristocrats and 'notables' set up 'provisional governments'. Sometimes these included a sprinkling of *capipopolo* and artisans, although most provisional governments were distinctly 'moderate' in composition. Indeed, there was little popular enthusiasm this time, and often no government left to revolt against. Further south there were distressingly few 'revolts', and where they did occur, as at Perugia, they were easily suppressed by Papal troops. In Umbria or the Marches no support came from outside, so after a few days people prudently took down their home-made Piedmontese flags and went home [54 *p. 215*].

In Emilia-Romagna, therefore, the patriotic 'moderates' took over during the early summer of 1859 – not because of any popular agitation, and certainly not because of any insurrectionary daring of their own, but because existing government had collapsed and the Piedmontese army was about to arrive. Admittedly their main aim was usually to protect public order and their own property, but they did take the initiative, they used the rhetoric of Italian unity, and they intended to hand power over, immediately and unconditionally, to Victor Emanuel. Luigi Farini became temporary 'dictator' of Modena and Parma; Bologna and the Romagna came under Colonel Leonetto Cipriani. 'Dictator' was sometimes an appropriate term. The new rulers censored the press and suppressed the Mazzinians just as enthusiastically as the old, although most of the exiles were permitted to return. They ran their regions as Piedmontese commissioners, i.e. as Cavour's agents, legitimized by the government in Turin. After Villafranca they could no longer claim this official link, but most of the local leaders stayed in office and the informal links to Piedmont remained. Central Italy, including the Papal Legations in Emilia-Romagna, was in Piedmontese hands, whatever Napoleon III and Francis Joseph might have decided at Villafranca, and whatever a European conference might decree in future.

So, too, was Tuscany, one of the few places where a genuine popular revolt had occurred – before the battle of Magenta, indeed even before the war began. On 27 April mass demonstrations erupted in Florence, led by the local republicans and by *capipopolo* like Dolfi. The National Society had had nothing to do with them. In fact, Cavour had been trying to bring Grand Duke Leopold into the anti-

Austrian alliance, and indeed early on 27 April Leopold did agree briefly to join the war and to appoint a 'liberal' government. However, he suddenly changed his mind and fled, much to the horror of the local 'moderates'. The best-known of them, Baron Ricasoli, hastily formed a provisional government to keep the republicans out. Unlike their counterparts in Emilia-Romagna, most of the Tuscan 'moderates' wanted to preserve Tuscan independence. But they feared the radicals in Florence and Livorno, and by mid-May, after some prompting from Cavour, Baron Ricasoli came round to the view that the best remedy against social unrest at home was 'annexation' to Piedmont. This was, of course, quite contrary to the Plombières agreement, let alone to Villafranca later, and also quite contrary to the original intentions of either Cavour or Napoleon III. Neither had supposed, before May 1859, that Piedmont might acquire Tuscany. If Leopold II had not fled on 27 April he would probably have remained Grand Duke, and Italian unification would not have occurred. Even after his flight many Tuscan 'moderates'. e.g. Ridolfi, despised the Piedmontese and thought Tuscan independence could be preserved, and Napoleon III remained hostile to any annexation [75 *p. 132*].

The whole of central Italy was now in Piedmontese hands, but not legitimately. The dukes had been driven out; the Pope had been deprived of his best lands. The La Marmora government of 1859–60 was not strong enough either to 'annexe' these territories, or to refuse them. A diplomatic stalemate ensued. Piedmont was dangerously isolated, apart from British support. But Austria had just been defeated in war, and was hardly likely to resume operations. Nor was Napoleon III, who had seen enough carnage. It was clearly time for bargaining. On 22 December a pamphlet was published in Paris, called *The Pope and the Congress*. It was written by La Guéronnière, on behalf of the Emperor. It argued that the Pope should be content with much smaller territories, and should certainly lose Emilia-Romagna. In other words, it was a signal: France would accept a Piedmontese takeover of the Legations.

On 20 January 1860 Cavour was reinstalled as Prime Minister, and struck a deal with the French. Piedmont would keep the central Italian duchies, including Tuscany, if their inhabitants voted for 'annexation' in plebiscites. In return, France would be given Savoy and Nice. The Treaty of Turin, in March, embodied this agreement. Cavour received French recognition of an expanded north-central Italian kingdom, much larger than anything envisaged at Plombières. France gained her 'natural frontiers' on the Alps, and some reward for her efforts in 1859. The losers, apart from Austria, were the Pope and the British. The Protestant British did not mind the Piedmontese taking over central Italy, especially from the Pope, and they had themselves pressed for plebiscites to legitimate the takeover; but they were furious about the French acquiring Savoy. Palmerston railed at Victor Emanuel for bargaining away the land 'that was the cradle of his family'. He also warned very strongly against any further concessions – rumour had it that the French were anxious to gain the island of Sardinia or even Liguria as well, and either would have been a real threat to British naval strength in the Mediterranean [*Doc. 14*].

The British veto saved Sardinia, if the French ever seriously wanted it. All that was left was to 'manage' the plebiscites carefully, to ensure they gave the right result both in central Italy (pro annexation to Piedmont) and in Savoy and Nice (pro annexation to France). The results, in all cases, were a triumph of creative electioneering, arguably the National Society's finest hour. All males aged 21 or over had the vote, for once (most of them never voted again). The plebiscites became a popular festival: bands played in the town squares, solemn processions marched to the polls, and free wine was distributed to the voters. Voting was, of course, in public, under the watchful eye of the National Guard. As most voters were illiterate, the ballot papers were sometimes distributed with 'yes' (*sí*) already printed on them; elsewhere local landowners helpfully offered the necessary help to their tenants (and in central Italy share-cropping was very common, so it was highly imprudent for a tenant to vote against his landlord's wishes). The choice was limited: either for 'annexation to the constitutional monarchy of King Victor Emanuel II', or for a vague 'separate kingdom' – it was deliberately left unclear whether this meant the return of the previous rulers.

In Tuscany, on 11–12 March 1860, the 'iron Baron' Ricasoli secured a vote of 386,445 to 14,925; in 'Emilia' (Modena, Parma, Bologna and the Legations) it was 427,512 to 756. Similar results were obtained the other way round in Savoy (130,583 to 235) and even in the Italian-speaking county of Nice (24,448 to 160), partly by having the polls closely supervised by the French army. Hitler and Stalin, in their heyday, never achieved results like this. *The Times*, on 30 April, described the Savoy plebiscite as 'the bitterest irony ever made on popular suffrage – the ballot box in the hands of the very authorities who issued the proclamation; no control possible; all opposition put down by intimidation'. But liberal honour was satisfied: the people had spoken. Victor Emanuel ruled thenceforth, at least in central Italy, not by God's grace but by the people's will. Only in Lombardy was a plebiscite not thought necessary, since the Lombards had already voted for annexation in 1848. Lombardy was incorporated into the Piedmontese state in November 1859 without a popular vote, but also without the 'Constituent Assembly' promised eleven years earlier.

By spring 1860, therefore, Piedmont had unexpectedly acquired most of north-central Italy except Venetia. But a French army still defended the Pope in Rome, and Napoleon III, fearing a Mediterranean rival, was by this time anxious to stop any further Piedmontese expansion. Moreover, Cavour was very unpopular at home because of the cession of Nice and Savoy: he could not even be sure that parliament would ratify it. At any rate, the war was clearly over. It was time to establish Piedmontese rule in the new provinces, and mend fences abroad.

GARIBALDI AND THE SOUTH

But in April came another unexpected shock. Giuseppe Garibaldi, the military 'Hero of Two Worlds', was furious that his own native town of Nice had been given away. He therefore planned an unofficial expedition, in the spirit of 'going it alone', in order to recapture it. Then came news of yet another anti-Bourbon insurrection in Palermo, and Garibaldi decided to liberate the Sicilians instead. He recruited a select group of volunteers, the famous 'Thousand' (actually at least 1,087, plus a few dozen more whose names are unknown). They were nearly all students or young professional men or artisans with a republican background, who had fought, or tried to fight, in the Piedmontese army in 1859. Three-quarters of them came from Lombardy, Liguria or Venetia; about 100 were southerners or Sicilians; not one was a peasant [16 *pp. 409–38*]. On 6 May 1860 they set off from Genoa. They were the latest of a long line of would-be northern liberators of the southern peasantry. Garibaldi, like many radicals and 'democrats' before him, believed that the south was the powder-keg of Italy, the natural centre of revolution. That is why he sailed – and this time it turned out to be true, at least in Sicily.

Cavour thought it was an insane scheme. How could a handful of student revolutionaries defeat a professional army? Moreover, he did not trust Garibaldi and his followers – they might attack Nice after all, or the Papal States. Hence initially he gave Garibaldi no backing, but he could not prevent the expedition. He was unpopular enough already, and there were a number of parliamentary by-elections coming up, as well as a parliamentary vote on Nice and Savoy. He also suspected the king was secretly backing the expedition, and knew that many army officers and officials supported it. He therefore turned a blind eye to Garibaldi's preparations. However, Cavour did prevent Garibaldi from acquiring decent weapons. Twelve thousand rifles, collected by the Million Rifles Fund organized by Bertani and stored in Milan, were blocked by government order. Garibaldi never forgave Cavour for this.

Garibaldi's expedition succeeded brilliantly, to everyone's surprise. His military lieutenants – Bixio, Sirtori, Medici, Cosenz – were highly competent, his political advisers like Crispi equally so. His men, equipped as they were only with rusty flintlocks that often would not fire, and with very little ammunition, were totally committed to the cause and greatly admired their commander. Discipline was severe and effective. Garibaldi managed to acquire some guns in Tuscany, en route to Sicily, and landed at Marsala in western Sicily on 11 May 1860. He recruited some local volunteers, and won his first – and, as it turned out, decisive – victory against the Neapolitan troops at Calatafimi four days later. The battle was won mainly by bayonet charges, for lack of guns and ammunition. He then pushed on to Palermo and took it on 26 May, just two weeks after landing. By early June Garibaldi was ruling most of western Sicily, in the name of Victor Emanuel. A further victory at Milazzo, on 20 July, gave him the eastern side of the island [*Doc. 15*].

It was one of the greatest military campaigns of all time, particularly as it was won by a thousand extremely ill-armed men. But Garibaldi did have some strokes of fortune. Unlike previous insurrectionaries, he did not need to foment revolt: there was one taking place already. Nearly all Sicilians, of all classes, detested the ill-disciplined Neapolitan troops, who were rarely paid and were given to looting. So the peasants supported Garibaldi, as they had not his predecessors, and this was vital in providing the local knowledge needed in war. In return, Garibaldi abolished the grist-tax, made some (ineffective) efforts to freeze prices, and issued a decree on 2 June promising a piece of municipal land to all who rose in arms.

But soon the peasants' revolt became too threatening. As the Bourbon police fled, the peasants began seizing land and murdering landowners. The middle and upper classes therefore organized their own protection squads, and turned to Garibaldi and Crispi for support. Garibaldi needed to give it, if he were to have any hope of running Sicily. So his regime soon became rather conservative. It paid rentiers their interest on (Bourbon) government bonds, it tried to conscript young men (at harvest time!), and it formed a militia – civic guards – to keep order in the towns. Above all, it suppressed peasant risings, most famously at the Nelson family estate of Bronte in early August. All this reassured the influential, and persuaded them that Victor Emanuel's regime might rule Sicily less badly, or at least preserve property more effectively, than the Bourbons had done.

These dramatic events were a shock to Cavour, but he reacted quickly. Garibaldi had, after all, invaded Sicily in the name of the king, and was proclaiming Italian unification. Most of his followers and volunteers might be radical republicans, but the general himself would probably stay loyal. He talked liberation, but he would deliver annexation. Cavour also knew that the National Society, after some initial hesitation, had backed Garibaldi's expedition and had provided some two hundred of the 'Thousand' on the original expedition. It now recruited more 'moderate' volunteers from all over Italy, who poured into Sicily and gave Garibaldi a sizeable army of at least 20,000 men, more than he needed. Cavour's strategy was clear. He would claim to have backed Garibaldi's plans all along, and would use the National Society to control any dangerous radicalism in Sicily. He allowed arms and money to flow south, and in June sent the Society's main organizer, the Sicilian La Farina, to Palermo as 'civil administrator' [*Doc. 16*]. However, La Farina had publicly supported the cession of Nice, and Garibaldi disliked him so much that after a few weeks he was thrown out of his own island, to be replaced by Agostino Depretis, a Piedmontese whom Garibaldi trusted.

Garibaldi, having conquered Sicily, could now cross to the southern mainland. Sicily was an excellent launchpad from which to assault the rest of southern Italy. On 19 August Garibaldi's troops crossed the Straits of Messina, with British connivance. They proceeded to defeat the Bourbon troops on the mainland as easily as they had done in Sicily. Helped, yet again, by peasant risings and the flight of Bourbon officials, Garibaldi marched up through the southern provinces and took Naples itself in early September, a mere three weeks after landing on the mainland. The new young king, Francis II, had fled the city. In early October Garibaldi defeated the demoralized Bourbon army at the decisive battle of the Volturno, near Caserta.

It was clear that the whole of southern Italy would now be annexed to Piedmont. Indeed, Cavour had to arrange 'annexation' quickly, or else leave the republicans and *Garibaldini* in control of the south. Hoping to legitimate a Piedmontese takeover, Cavour had tried hard to provoke a rising in Naples before Garibaldi arrived but, as usual, his revolutionary schemes had failed [*Doc. 17*]. The Neapolitans proved unaccountably reluctant to rise against the intolerable Bourbon yoke. In September they welcomed Garibaldi as a hero, but were highly unenthusiastic about 'Italy' or the Piedmontese, and gave Victor Emanuel a very lukewarm reception when he arrived in November. The kingdom of Naples, in short, played virtually no part in the final, crucial period of Italian unification. It was simply conquered, mostly by republican 'democrats'; it was then handed over to 'moderate' northerners – northerners who had never wanted to rule the south, and who had certainly not fought for it. Piedmont acquired it not because the Neapolitans themselves wanted that outcome, nor because of any feat of arms by the Piedmontese army, but because a great guerrilla leader and military genius so decided.

On 21 October plebiscites were held both on the mainland and in Sicily. They were even more farcical than the ones in central Italy had been, since no alternative was on offer: you voted 'yes' or 'no' to 'One Italy Victor Emanuel'. This had been Garibaldi's slogan, and most people probably voted for or against Garibaldi rather than 'Italy'. In Sicily, 432,053 voted 'yes', and 667 against; in the Kingdom of Naples, it was 1,302,064 to 10,312. So the south was annexed, and Piedmontese officials could be sent in. This was not a successful move. Garibaldi's men in September-October 1860 had not been great administrators in Naples, but the Piedmontese incomers proved even worse. They soon became very unpopular. Problems were building up for the future.

CROSSING THE RUBICON

Garibaldi's real target was not Naples but Rome. Cavour had failed to prevent Garibaldi taking Naples, but at all costs he had to stop Garibaldi's 'march on Rome'. An attack on Rome risked drawing Piedmont into a war against the French, whose troops were in Rome to protect the Pope, and perhaps into renewed war against the Austrians as well. And this would jeopardize all Piedmont's recent gains. Moreover, if Garibaldi conquered Rome the 'democrats' and republicans would win even more prestige than they had already. It would be obvious to all that they, not Piedmont and Victor Emanuel, had united Italy. Garibaldi, although loyal so far, was not exactly a committed royalist, and his followers would certainly demand a Constituent Assembly, if not a republic. Cavour's answer to these problems was simple, and by now familiar. Revolts would break out in the Papal States against clerical misrule. The insurrectionaries would invite the Piedmontese to take over. The army would then invade the Papal States from the north, would skirt round Rome itself, and would 'link up with', i.e. intercept, Garibaldi's troops moving up from Naples. Garibaldi's advance would be halted, the Pope would keep the city of Rome, Napoleon III would be kept happy, and Piedmont would acquire yet more territory – Umbria and the Marches.

Needless to say, this plan misfired at stage one. Despite all the efforts of Cavour's agents, revolts yet again failed to materialize, except in one or two towns like Orvieto and Urbino. Piedmont therefore had little option but to invade the Marches anyway, and did so on 11 September. She then found herself fighting the Pope and taking over his territory, without a declaration of war and without any provocation or conceivable justification, except the rather feeble one that Garibaldi would have done the same thing more successfully. Even so, the strategy worked in the end. Piedmontese troops, led initially by General Cialdini and in the later stages by Victor Emanuel himself, moved quickly through the Marches. Napoleon III, never anxious to fight Garibaldi, did not make a move; nor did the Austrians. All the Papal States, except Latium and the city of Rome itself, were taken over with tacit French acquiescence.

In early November came the plebiscites, held once again in a festive, self-congratulatory fervour. Bishops threatened peasants with excommunication if they voted for Piedmont; landlords threatened them with eviction if they did not. Eviction was a more serious threat. The Marches, now run by prominent figures in the National Society, voted 133,765 to 1,212 to join 'Italy one and indivisible under our constitutional sovereign Victor Emanuel'. Umbria, with more sharecroppers, was even more enthusiastic: 97,040 to 360 [54 *p. 387*].

By this time troops led by Victor Emanuel had joined up with those under Garibaldi. On 26 October the two men met at Teano, on the Naples frontier. Their handshake symbolized the creation of a united 'Italy' – and the nature of the new regime. By unofficial initiative and brilliant tactical generalship, Garibaldi had won Sicily and the south for his king. But the real winner was Cavour. Garibaldi, or the French, won the battles; Cavour won the war – or, at least, the spoils of war, although in southern Italy they turned out to be disappointingly troublesome. Cavour both conciliated and outmanoeuvred the French emperor, and made Italian unification acceptable throughout Europe. He prevented Garibaldi from taking Rome, but himself took over most of the Papal States, without a diplomatic furore. He completely pre-empted the Mazzinians at home, and he managed to get rid of Nice and Savoy without too much protest – except from

Garibaldi. It was a triumph of imaginative statecraft, comparable only to Garibaldi's triumphs on the battlefield. In a dozen years Cavour and his few supporters had turned a minor, rather reactionary little state into a united Italian kingdom, run by safe, reliable men with liberal views and a decent respect for their king, and recognized by all as a European Power [*Doc. 18*].

9 UNITED AT LAST?

After 1861 Venice and Rome remained outside the new Kingdom of Italy, each occupied or protected by a major European Power. The republicans were furious. In their view Victor Emanuel had thrown away the first needlessly at Villafranca, and Cavour had deliberately prevented Garibaldi from taking the second. But by this time no-one seriously believed that the two would not be annexed sooner or later, probably sooner. Indeed, by January 1861 Cavour was still trying to bribe Cardinal Antonelli, the Papal Secretary of State, to let Italy have Rome in return for a payment of three million lire p.a. to the Pope and the Curia, and fifteen million to Antonelli personally [76 *p. 246*]. This improbable scheme was bound to fail, particularly when thousands of monks and friars were being evicted from their monasteries all over central and southern Italy. But the Papal hold on Rome was obviously precarious. The Pope had few troops of his own, and even though the French garrison remained in the city, Napoleon III was manifestly reluctant to use it. Garibaldi's followers were spoiling for another invasion, and Cavour himself declared that the capital city of the new Italy should be Rome. As for Venetia, in 1865 an Italian government offered to buy it from the Austrians for 100 million lire, but the Austrians refused [34 *p. 122*].

In 1862 Garibaldi attempted to repeat his 1860 exploits. Crossing from Sicily again with another volunteer force, and with tacit support from the Rattazzi government and the king, he intended to march on Rome. But the government's role became embarrassingly public knowledge, and the diplomatic repercussions looked threatening. Italian troops had to be used to stop him. At the battle of Aspromonte the hero of Italian unification, the man who had handed over all southern Italy to his king two years earlier, was defeated – and wounded – by the king's army.

If neither bribery nor guerrilla war worked, perhaps diplomacy might. In September 1864 Minghetti's government made a secret agreement with Napoleon III that French troops would withdraw from Rome within two years. In return, the Italians promised that they would not attack the city. As proof of their good intentions, they would make Florence the capital of Italy. The Pope would be allowed to recruit a 10,000-strong army to defend his territories. This last provision was particularly absurd, since the Pope could not afford such a force, nor would it be effective against the Italian army even if he could. When news leaked out, there were major riots in the existing capital, Turin, at the loss of capital status: 50 people were killed. Nonetheless, in 1865 the Italian government and bureaucracy decamped to Florence, and set about destroying the city centre in order to build its offices. In December 1866 the French duly withdrew from Rome. This was virtually an open invitation to Garibaldi. The next year he gathered another invading force, once more with the tacit support of a Rattazzi government. This time his 3,000 volunteers were defeated by Papal troops. They were then beaten more comprehensively at the battle of Mentana by the French, who had rushed back hastily to help the Pope [*Doc. 19*]. Thereafter a French garrison remained, rather reluctantly, at the Papal port of Civitavecchia until 1870. Napoleon III did not wish to defend the Temporal Power, and of course the French garrison ruined his relations with the Italian government, but he had little option given the strength of Catholic opinion at home.

Yet again, war succeeded where diplomacy had failed. In 1866 the Italian government signed a military alliance with the Prussians. Bismarck, the Prussian Chancellor, was preparing to attack Austria, and wanted a second front in Italy. Venetia would be the reward for a successful war. The Austrians, learning of this, offered Venetia to Italy, if Italy and France stayed neutral in the coming war. Since Napoleon III had no wish to join the war anyway, he readily agreed. But the La Marmora government refused, partly because of its promise to Bismarck, but mainly because it suspected that if Austria beat Prussia she would go back on her word.

Thus began one of the most ludicrous and pointless wars in history. Italy could have acquired Venetia anyway, without fighting; Austrian troops fought to retain territory which their government had been perfectly willing to give away. Both sides were fighting not for Venetia, but for their honour. The Italians' military honour did not last long. The Austrians beat the Italians both on land, at the second battle of Custoza (June 1866) and, especially, at sea, where they overwhelmingly defeated a larger Italian fleet at Lissa (Vis), in the Adriatic, and sank the Italian admiral's flagship. Both Italian defeats showed an unusual degree of military incompetence and lack of foresight. Nonetheless, north of the Alps the Prussians won the war, defeating the Austrians at the battle of Sadowa. So Italy acquired Venetia after all, once the inevitable rigged plebiscites had been held – 642,000 in favour of annexation, 69 against, a result that surpassed all previous electoral triumphs. But it had been acquired ingloriously, after thousands of needless deaths. It was a farcical postscript to the romantic battles of the earlier unification period.

In 1870 this improbable set of circumstances was repeated. This time it was the French who found themselves faced with a war against Bismarck. Italy remained neutral, but only because the government forced the king to break his promise of support to Napoleon III. The French emperor naturally had to withdraw his troops from Rome to help on the Rhine, so the city was left virtually defenceless. In September 1870, after the Prussian victory at Sedan, Giovanni Lanza's Italian government sent its army into Rome. Despite token resistance by the Papal troops – nineteen of them were killed, and 49 Italians – the city was soon taken. Despite Mazzini's efforts, popular insurrection was conspicuously absent, as it had been in Venetia four years earlier – indeed, Italian troops received an extremely lukewarm welcome both in Venice and in Rome. A plebiscite followed: 133,681 to 1,507. Rome was proclaimed capital of Italy, this time to the fury of the Florentines. Pius IX yet again denounced the new kingdom and the total loss of his territories, and declared himself to be a 'prisoner in the Vatican'. Italy was unified at last, but she had alienated the Church. Even then Trentino and Julian Venetia (Trieste), regarded as equally 'Italian' even by many in government, remained in Austrian hands until 1918, much to the disgust of Garibaldi and his volunteers who had spent the 1866 war fighting there.

PIEDMONTISATION ALL ROUND

The man who had perhaps done most to create the new Italy did not live to see this outcome. On 6 June 1861 Cavour died unexpectedly, at the age of fifty, probably of a malarial fever. The new kingdom thus lost its one great statesman, less than three months after parliament had proclaimed Victor Emanuel II as 'King of Italy'. Note that the king was, and remained, Victor Emanuel *the Second*, a title deliberately chosen in order to emphasize that the new Italy was the old Piedmont, made larger by 'annexations'; and he was proclaimed by the *eighth* parliament, not the first. Indeed, all the formal institutions of the new state were those of Piedmont. The other regions were forced to adopt Piedmontese laws, to pay Piedmontese taxes, and to be ruled by (mainly) Piedmontese officials. And Piedmont, with its government appointment of mayors and its centrally-appointed prefects in charge of provincial administration and local government, had a strong centralizing tradition based on service to the crown. Even the capital remained in Turin until 1865.

The unitary nature of the new state was actually decided in autumn 1859, before unification, and rather fortuitously. While Cavour was temporarily out of office after Villafranca, the La Marmora government found it had to administer newly-acquired Lombardy while its attention was mostly directed to diplomacy and war. The Interior Minister, Rattazzi, who personally strongly favoured the 'French' model of central administration and control of local government familiar in Piedmont, simply applied it to Lombardy by emergency decree, without any parliamentary debate. The Lombards were furious, particularly as they had been promised a Constituent Assembly back in 1848. Half the Lombard members of the National Society resigned, complaining that the new legislation was worse than that of the Austrians. The Lombards lost their governor, their traditional local councils and their established systems of education, justice and public security. Exactly the same happened in Emilia-Romagna too, in 1859–60. The 'dictator', Farini, came from Modena and had no wish to see any 'Emilian' autonomy, since it would have meant rule by the hated Bolognese. In both Lombardy and Emilia-Romagna the Piedmontese legal codes were applied virtually overnight. Tuscany, however, was rather different. It had politically powerful landowners (Baron Ricasoli was Cavour's successor as Prime Minister in 1861), it had enlightened legal codes and it had a strong free-trade tradition. Hence it could resist Piedmontisation, at least temporarily: the Tuscans retained their own criminal code and Court of Appeal for a time, as well as their own issue banks [72 p. 42; 75 pp. 248–74].

By autumn 1860 there was, in fact, much grumbling in the regions. Nearly all liberals in other regions welcomed some aspects of Piedmontese rule – the Constitution and its guarantee of civil liberties, an elected parliament – but they strongly disliked losing their administrative and legal traditions and their own local government. They also disliked the Piedmontese officials personally, particularly the prefects, and they objected to the tough police powers imposed in October 1859. Cavour had to promise both the Sicilians and the Neapolitans their own regional self-government, with their own elected assemblies and administrations, a promise he reneged on after the plebiscites. To placate the discontent, both Farini and (especially) Minghetti, as Ministers of the Interior, produced rather feeble schemes for regional devolution throughout Italy. There would be regional governors (appointed by central government) and administrations, and regional assemblies, chosen by provincial councillors, with powers over major public works and higher education; there would also be elected mayors at municipal level. But in 1861 parliament rejected all this very firmly. It was too great a threat to the new, fragile national unity.

Moreover, by this time Piedmont had taken over Sicily and the mainland south, and had begun to realize what conditions were like down there. It was obvious that if the new Italy was going to provide any decent government or administration in the south, then both political power and administrative or judicial jobs had to be removed from the local elites; any kind of self-government would be disastrous. To good liberals, this seemed equally true in Venetia after 1866, where the local populace was distressingly clerical and very hostile, for example, to the law on civil marriage; and in Rome itself after 1870. So centralization was the only answer. The Piedmontese administrative system and Piedmontese laws, including on such matters as local government, schooling, civil marriage and church property, were applied generally throughout the whole of Italy in 1861 (and approved by parliament only four years later, even then with minimal debate). Sicilian peasants became liable for conscription, Piedmontese taxes had to be paid, and low Piedmontese tariffs destroyed thousands of southern artisan jobs.

Throughout the Risorgimento period many respected writers, both 'neo-guelph' and republican, had argued for regionalism or federalism. Many battles had been fought in 1848–9, and even in 1859–60, essentially for regional motives and regional autonomy. Even the agreement at Plombières in 1858 had envisaged a confederal Italy. Yet the ultimate outcome was quite different. One reason was that Italian politicians were concerned about their own municipalities, not their 'regions', let alone regions elsewhere. Cavour, for example, a well-travelled man by nineteenth-century standards, only visited Tuscany once in his life and never went further south, not even to Rome or Naples; he did not visit Sardinia even though the island had been ruled from Turin since 1720 and its affairs were regularly discussed there. But the main reason was that except in Tuscany the regional elites could not negotiate with the Piedmontese from a position of strength. Most of them needed the Piedmontese more than the Piedmontese needed them. In the south, the old landowning elites had played little part in expelling the Bourbons, feared the local peasantry and hoped that the Piedmontese security forces would protect their property. Only the Sicilians, with a reasonably powerful elite, drew up a scheme in late 1860 for regional devolution with a legislative council, but the Piedmontese ignored it. The Sicilians, greatly relieved to be rid of the Neapolitan yoke, did not protest too much, at least initially.

Italian governments were usually less concerned about the civil service or legal system than about the army. In 1860 the key political question was how to absorb the armies of the former independent states, and the Garibaldine volunteers, into the regular Italian army. The answer, at least for the Bourbon army of Naples, was to take the officers in, with the same rank and full pay, and to dismiss the ordinary soldiers – who promptly took to the hills and became armed brigands. As for Garibaldi's volunteers, they had been far more successful than the official armies in 1859–60, and consequently had to be disbanded, except for the 'Thousand' who were so famous they had to be given army posts if they so wished (few did). Even Garibaldi himself, the greatest military genius since Napoleon I, was sidelined. He was furious at the way his men had been treated, and denounced Cavour very publicly in parliament. This was, indeed, one of the reasons why he was so bitterly opposed to the Italian governments of those years, and why he was so willing to fight on unofficially against the Austrians. Even so, the army clearly became less 'Piedmontese', and less aristocratic, after 1861. By 1872 only 9 per cent of the officers were noblemen: by 1887 only 3 per cent. This was true of most other state institutions too, except for the diplomatic corps [85 *p. 428*].

THE SOUTHERN QUESTION

In the 1860s the army had a real job to do. In much of the mainland south and Sicily public order had collapsed with the end of the Bourbon regime. Piedmontese efforts to restore it were unwelcome. Brigands, sometimes operating in bands of around 20 men, became extremely common, their numbers swollen by ex-soldiers from the Bourbon army, by reluctant conscripts to the Italian one and by criminals who had escaped from unguarded prisons in 1860. Essentially they were local gangs. There was very little political or military co-ordination between them, unlike in the 1790s, and they had no ideology except a wish to return to the good old days and to the erstwhile collective rights of the poor. A particular grievance was the sale of Church lands, which wrecked the existing welfare system. The brigands murdered 'collaborating' local officials, fought against mayors and councillors, and were used by the more unscrupulous landowning families in local disputes and vendettas. The south, in short, revolted against the new order, not only through brigandage but also through years of tax strikes, urban riots, desertion, arson and land occupations. It all culminated in a major anti-government rising in Palermo in 1866.

The Piedmontese answer to all this was simple: send in the army. Over 100,000 troops were moved down south, not only to repress the 'brigands' but also to purge the local judiciary and make sure local landowners and councillors understood the message: dissent, from any group, would not be tolerated. Martial law was imposed by military tribunals, and summary executions followed. More people were killed in these years of 'brigandage' than in all the battles of the unification struggle put together [*Doc. 20*]. By the late 1860s 'brigandage' had been mostly wiped out, and governments began to make concessions to the local elites, distrusted though they still were. But it had been a traumatic few years, and left a legacy that is still manifest today. The 'progressive', northern 'liberals' had taken over the south. They had immediately reneged on their promises of administrative 'autonomy', and thus alienated middle-class officials and lawyers, as well as many influential landowners. They had then been faced with a spontaneous and very widespread peasants' revolt, and their only response had been to persecute many of the southern gentry and to massacre the southern peasants. It was a dreadful record. Even the Bourbons had never behaved like that.

Most northern liberals and radicals had, of course, applauded the army's actions. The authority of the new state had to be established, and peasant revolt put down. So it was, but the cost was high. Northerners came to despise their southern fellow-citizens as superstitious and barbaric; southerners resented and detested their arrogant northern rulers. d'Azeglio called the union of northern Italy with Naples 'like going to bed with someone who has smallpox' [*75 p. 273*]. Perhaps Italian unification had not been such a good idea after all.

ONE AND INDIVISIBLE

The new State had other problems too. It had been founded by men expecting greater prosperity from a larger market and lower tariffs. Yet the public finances were dreadful. In 1861 the Italian national debt was 2.5 billion lire, at least half of it inherited from the Kingdom of Sardinia and its recent wars, and this debt grew rapidly in the next decade. The annual budget deficit was around 400 million lire, about the same as the total *revenue* of all the previous Italian states. Despite privatization receipts from sale of Church and crown lands, for decades to come the interest on the national debt swallowed up nearly half the state's revenues. Military spending took another quarter, and could not be cut in the 1860s as Rome and Venice were still to be won. The wars of 1866 and 1870, short and inglorious as they were, proved very expensive. To most of its citizens, therefore, the new Italy meant not independence, nor unity, nor liberty, nor civil rights. It meant high taxes, low welfare and compulsory military service. In 1868–9 there were riots all over Italy against the new grist-tax on milling; 267 people were killed.

However, the state's financial problems had one huge advantage: they made war less likely. King Victor Emanuel II insisted on being military commander-in-chief himself, preened himself on the glorious military traditions of the House of Savoy, and appointed the ministers of war and the navy. He also meddled constantly in foreign policy, usually taking a bellicose line that his embarrassed ministers somehow had to play down. The Constitution gave him the right to make war and peace. Occasionally, as in 1864, he appointed a general to be prime minister, in the hope of a good war. This was a highly dangerous situation, made more dangerous by the death of Cavour. The new Italy might easily have been dragged down by military defeat, and partitioned again by the victors. If this did not happen, it was largely due to luck, and to lack of money.

So the new state survived, precariously. By the late 1860s it was beginning to reconcile the various regional elites, and bring them together into its key institutions – the army, the civil service, parliament. Admittedly the parliamentary electorate was small, about 418,000 people, around 2 per cent of the population, and 44,000 of these were employees of central or local government. But they were the key people in the country, and they had the vote. This meant that in practice 'Piedmontese' rule was mitigated; it could not be as centralist as all that. Governments who ignored parliamentary deputies would lose key parliamentary votes, and soon collapse; deputies who ignored local interests would not be re-elected. They soon became spokesmen for constituency and even regional issues, pushing through legislation favouring their own region.

Moreover, local government remained the real focus of Italian political life. It was local, not national, government that decided most taxes, controlled jobs, and allocated land. By the late 1860s it was usually the same people running it as before, even in the south. Mayors were in principle appointed centrally, but in practice the choice was made by the prefect, who had to choose a local land-owner, and furthermore one who could deliver the vote to the pro-government candidate at the next parliamentary election. Hence the prefect usually had very little choice at all, nor any real influence over local government. Powerful local landowners and 'notables' con-trolled the vote, controlled local government, built up a solid support from numerous hangers-on and 'clients', elected the deputy and won favours from compliant governments. The southern landowners and middle class learned to work the system and became reconciled to it, if never enthusiastic. This was 'centralization Italian-style' – totally dependent on local elites. Despite the efforts of its rulers, the new Italy was not Greater Piedmont after all [39, 102].

PART THREE: ASSESSMENT

10 CONCLUSION

By September 1870 Rome was taken, and Italian 'unification' was complete, although Trentino, South Tyrol and the Trieste region remained in Austrian hands until 1918, and Garibaldi's native Nice remains French to this day. The dual process, of 'expelling the foreigner' and 'uniting the peninsula' had been remarkably quick – just over two decades, if one starts from the accession of Pius IX in 1846; a mere twelve years, if one regards the Plombières agreement of 1858 as the starting point.

It was an astonishing achievement, made possible by extraordinary good fortune and by the complementary gifts of two men of genius, Cavour and Garibaldi. The Crimean War left Austria friendless; and most of the existing Italian states depended on Austria. Cavour, playing on Napoleon III's ambition and on his romantic streak, secured the Franco-Piedmontese alliance and the war of 1859 against Austria, and won Lombardy; later foreign wars, in 1866 and 1870, brought Venice and Rome. Much of the actual fighting for Italian unity was done by foreigners: one estimate is that only 6,000 Italians died in all the wars of the Risorgimento put together, whereas 7,668 Frenchmen were killed in 1859 alone [75 p. 36].

But 'national sentiment' and popular insurrections were vital too, and not only in 1848. It was the 'moderate'-led revolts of mid-1859 in central Italy that made Italian unification, as opposed to a north Italian kingdom of the kind agreed at Plombières, possible. And it was Garibaldi's genius and determination that won the south in 1860, and forced Cavour to annexe it before Garibaldi could march on Rome. Garibaldi, with his immense courage and his selfless nobility of soul, epitomized the heroic, self-sacrificing drama of the Risorgimento – after all, tens of thousands of ordinary Italians volunteered to risk their lives and fight for 'Italy'. Moreover, these volunteer amateurs achieved far more spectacular victories than Victor Emanuel's army ever managed to do. Indeed, the Piedmontese army 'conquered' only Lombardy, Umbria and the Marches (and the first of these only with a great deal of French help), whereas Garibaldi and his 'Thousand' became a legend throughout the world.

Even so, I stress that the Risorgimento was not a 'national insurrection', even in 1848–9. 'National' sentiment was restricted to a small, educated urban minority. Even in most of the northern and central Italian cities the people obstinately refused to revolt in 1859–60, despite all the frantic efforts of Cavour and the National Society. Serious political discontent was confined to Sicily (where it was directed against Naples, not Austria) and to the Papal Legations of Emilia-Romagna. Revolts, when they did occur, were local in kind, caused by taxes or land sales rather than by any desire for 'independence'. Some regions – for example, Sardinia – were not affected by war or revolt at all. Others, including the whole of the mainland south, were simply conquered.

The Constitution of the new Italian State after 1861 was that of Piedmont, granted by Charles Albert in 1848. No Constituent Assembly was summoned, nor was there any great Italian lawgiver like Washington or Napoleon. Italy's new rulers, at least until 1876, were a 'moderate' elite of aristocrats and landowners, initially mostly Piedmontese, Tuscans, or Emilians, later augmented by Sicilians. These were the real winners of the 1846–61 struggles. They came mostly from those regions of Italy where the landowning elites had, in the early part of the century, retained their land and much of their social prestige and political power. Elsewhere local elites remained distinctly unenthusiastic about the new state. This was not surprising. Italy's king, army, parliament, administrative and judicial system, laws, schooling, currency, taxes and tariffs were all 'Piedmontese' – a term that soon came to signify, to Italians from other regions, not 'liberal' or 'constitutional', but 'impersonal' and 'centralizing', or even 'militarist' and 'oppressive'.

Indeed, many people soon became remarkably hostile to the new Kingdom of Italy. In the mainland south, resistance ('brigandage') lasted for at least five years and was only crushed by the army. Garibaldi himself, still furious about the loss of Nice, denounced the outcome, took up arms again and by 1862 was wounded in battle against Italian troops. Mazzini, the prophet and apostle of Italian unity, lamented that 'I had hoped to evoke the soul of Italy, and instead find merely the inanimate corpse' [77 p. 212]. Cattaneo, still a republican and federalist, described the new state as a 'royal conquest', an annexation by the only Italian state with an army. His friend Ferrari thought big states were inevitably oppressive bureaucracies, like Russia or China; the Italians should have taken

Switzerland, not France, as the model. This 'democratic' opposition remained very significant. The 'democrats' had, after all, regarded Italian unification as their own project. Yet they felt cheated by the outcome. Thereafter there was always an alternative, radical and republican opposition to the official Italy of Victor Emanuel (which was one reason why the monarchy never became a focus of national loyalty). This opposition could reasonably claim to have played a vital role in bringing the new state into existence, and it was prepared to take up arms again.

But it was not only the 'democrats' who were unhappy after 1861. The Catholic Church, and her adherents throughout the country, were also among the big losers of the Risorgimento. Pius IX had been prominent in the 'national' movement in 1846–7, but had broken with it in 1848. Thereafter the Risorgimento was essentially secularizing. The Church lost not only the Papal States and Rome itself (apart from a small area round the Vatican, and even that was formally 'Italian' territory until 1929) but most of her lands and revenues as well. Many religious orders were closed down, and over 4,000 monasteries and convents were taken over by the new lay state. Education and charities were taken over too, and became municipal, or state, responsibilities. In much of the south, where the Church was often based not on parishes but on local ecclesiastical communities, her entire structure was destroyed. Pius IX proclaimed himself to be a 'prisoner in the Vatican'; his complaints were echoed by 130,000 clergy throughout the land, and by millions of ordinary Catholics. All this had major political consequences. The new state, with its capital in clerical Rome, was fragile. It needed the backing of the Church, but its domestic policies made that impossible. Here was the essential weakness of the new Italy, and explains why Italian politicians, for decades to come, remained obsessed by Church-state relations.

The rural poor were also big losers. If they had not already lost their traditional grazing rights and common land to enclosures, they certainly did so after 1861, and were subjected to heavy land taxes and conscription as well. The Risorgimento, to many peasants in the north as well as the south, meant godless landowners grabbing the vital resources of the poor, and controlling all access to welfare. The peasants, indeed, had been the great absentees of the Risorgimento campaigns. Not a single peasant sailed with Garibaldi to Sicily; when he arrived, he found the local peasants in revolt, but not for 'Italy'. Rural uprisings and riots had of course occurred over land tenure and taxes before 1861, but they became more common later. In other words, the peasants – the majority of the Italian population – had

had relatively few grievances against the old regimes, but they had plenty against the new one, which attacked their traditional rights and customs with unprecedented zeal.

In the towns, too, the craftsmen and artisans were now exposed to virtual free trade, and often could not compete with foreign factory producers. Nor could much domestic industry in rural zones, or even some of the major industries, like shipbuilding and engineering at Naples. Arguably the south would have prospered more as an independent state; it could have devalued its currency, and thus priced its workers back into jobs. As it was, its industry and much of its agriculture were destroyed after 1861, while public order collapsed over land disputes and local government abuses. Local elite members, particularly landowners, were also badly hit, and in the south often felt despised and ignored by the Piedmontese. Eventually, thanks to their control of local government, patronage and the parliamentary vote, the southerners learned to work the system, but that simply displaced the problem: by the 1890s Lombardy had become a centre of disaffection against the new regime, which it perceived as dominated by southerners.

Yet the new state, bureaucratic and over-centralized as it was, somehow survived. 'Unification', in some form, had seemed desirable to many influential Italians in the 1840s and continued to seem so decades later. 'Italy' may have been the work of a tiny minority, but it had a certain logic. The Italian state could appeal to the glorious past, to cultural nationalism; and it could also embrace fashionable concepts of 'progress' or (by the 1880s) colonialism. It provided greater opportunities for the ambitious professional classes; it protected basic civil liberties, at least for the educated urban laity, and some degree of political representation; and it ensured domestic economic integration and a larger market-based economy, which might have hurt the vested interests of small artisans but also opened up hugely profitable new perspectives for the commercial elite. Above all, the new state protected its citizens' property, and its land privatization programme offered the chance of adding to it. Many of its opponents became reconciled: Garibaldi himself was a deputy in the Italian parliament, and Church opposition softened with time.

Italian unification, in the form it took in 1861, was certainly an unexpected accident; but after 1861 it seemed, in retrospect, an accident that had been waiting to happen. In the last resort the Kingdom of Italy was created, and survived, because of the 'progressive' ideas on economic, social, cultural and religious matters current at the time among the educated elite, particularly the professional classes and the more liberal lesser nobility. It was these men, not the 'bourgeoisie' in any commercial or Marxist sense, who wanted change. They disseminated their ideas through journalism, scientific congresses, freemasonry, informal networks and cafe society. After 1870, once Rome was taken and schooling spread throughout the peninsula, their ideas were inculcated more widely both among the various regional elites and among ordinary people. The liberal historian Benedetto Croce praised this process as the work of 'a spiritual aristocracy of upright and loyal gentlemen' [36 *p. 5*]; more cynically, one might see it as the work of a self-interested elite in control of propaganda. At any rate, the unification of Italy and the survival of the new kingdom after 1861 both depended on the Risorgimento – a cultural revival, but above all an economic-social programme for transforming society in a 'modern', 'progressive', 'European' manner.

Italy's European partners naturally approved. The French did much of the fighting; and many of the new regime's ideas and administrative structures were taken directly from France. The British were even more delighted. Unification set up a parliamentary monarchy (the only one on the continent, among the larger Powers), run by liberal-sounding Anglophile gentlemen, open to free trade and therefore to British products, reassuringly anti-Popish and likely to be a useful Mediterranean ally. No wonder British historians have given the Risorgimento such a good press.

However, in another sense Italy was not united at all. Italian society – the 'real country' – remained diverse, and many Italians remained remarkably hostile to the new kingdom. By the late nineteenth century Italy had one of the strongest and most violent anarchist movements in Europe, and in 1900 an anarchist assassinated the king. Most people still spoke only dialect, and almost half were still illiterate in 1900. The Fascist regime of 1922–45 may be seen as a further attempt to unify Italian society and build a 'nation', but it, too, largely failed.

Only in the last few decades have Italians come to have some recognizable – although highly Americanized, or 'global' – common culture. But this has coincided with regional devolution in the 1970s and with the rise of strong regionalist and federal movements in northern Italy, hostile to the institutions and to the very concept of a united Italy. It has coincided, too, with the growth of European economic and political integration. A host of key decisions – on defence, foreign policy, economic regulation, agriculture, even the currency – are no longer taken by the Italian state set up in 1861. That state has been eroded, as it was created, both from above and from below. So

Italian unification now appears in a more prosaic light. Perhaps it was not the glorious achievement of a manifest destiny after all. At any rate, it was certainly not the end of the story.

PART FOUR: DOCUMENTS

DOCUMENT 1   HOW THE FUTURE OF CENTRAL ITALY
WAS DECIDED IN 1815

Cardinal Ercole Consalvi was Pope Pius VII's envoy at the Congress of Vienna in 1814–15, charged with securing the return of the Papal States. He here reports to Rome a discussion with Prince Metternich in Vienna, on the restoration of Papal rule in central Italy.

Starting as always from his principle that we are being given the Legations, not having them restored to us, the Prince told me that Ferrara is being given on condition that Austrian garrisons should be permanently stationed both there and at Comacchio. I objected to this on the grounds that the Pope was an independent sovereign, but this objection was not considered valid since clearly a donor is permitted to stipulate conditions to his gift. I also objected on the grounds of the Holy See's neutrality. I argued that in peacetime these garrisons would be useless, but in time of war Austria, as a neighbouring country, was in a position to occupy them before anyone else did, and could ignore the protests that we would make in the name of our neutrality; nor did I fail to tell him that, for Austria's greater security, we would be willing to agree verbally to this now. But he replied that the Pope's neutrality would be compromised anyway if Austria occupied these fortresses in time of war, for the other belligerent Powers would not be impressed by a simple protest by the Pope, nor regard his duties as a neutral as being fulfilled by that act alone ... the Prince added that we should find a word to describe them properly, and after thinking for a while said 'I think we should call them "frontier fortresses" (*forteresses de barrière*)'. ...

The Prince then went on to another subject, i.e. the system of government to be set up in the Legations. He started from the principle that these three provinces, accustomed for about twenty-five years now to a system of government very different from Papal rule, and being furthermore full of hotheads reluctant to be ruled once again by priests, could not possibly be brought under the old system of government, nor under the same kind of rule as the other Papal provinces. He said that it was important for the peace of all Italy that unrest should be avoided in the towns of central Italy, which were in contact with Lombardy and the Venetian States. He added that the Powers were unanimously agreed on this article, and that it was indispensable to find and agree on a different kind of government for these provinces ... in my reply I established first of all a basic principle: whatever the Holy Father was obliged by necessity to do in the three Legations, he would have to do in all the rest of his States, since if for example something was granted in Ravenna it was impossible that demands for equal treatment would not be raised in Ancona, Macerata, Perugia and above all in Rome, especially given the people's present way of thinking. We should not deceive ourselves by supposing otherwise, and should keep this in mind while deciding what to do in the Legations. The Prince was convinced by this evident truth ... I pointed out that if a sort of Constitution was set up in the Legations (and hence in the rest of the Papal States, as I have already shown), Naples, Tuscany, Lombardy, Venetia and Piedmont would have of necessity to do the same, and it did not seem to me certain that this was in the interest of the Emperor or of the other sovereigns. He agreed, and so this was ruled out.

The other point was about employing laymen in the government. On this point, which the Allies regard as very important, I said that I personally did not disagree within certain limits ... (but) it would be impossible not to do the same thing for the whole of the State, including Rome ... and Papal government by its very nature has certain features that cannot be changed without virtually overthrowing the government itself. It is, therefore, I said, impossible to admit laymen into government posts to the degree that is normal in a secular State. But this does not mean it cannot be done to some extent as need arises ... however, decisions of this kind should not be taken by the Congress, so as to preserve the dignity of the Holy Father and to ensure that his subjects are obliged to him and not to the Congress ... the Prince showed that he was impressed by these sensible arguments, and I believe that on this very serious issue matters will rest in the terms outlined.

Cardinal Consalvi to Cardinal Pacca, acting Secretary of State, 9 May 1815, in A. Roveri *et al.* (eds), *La Missione Consalvi e il Congresso di Vienna*, iii, Istituto Storico Italiano per l'Età Moderna e Contemporanea, Rome 1973, pp. 519–22.

DOCUMENT 2   CARLO CATTANEO CELEBRATES HIS
              NATIVE LOMBARDY

Cattaneo was an extraordinarily erudite writer with a very wide range of scientific and historical interests. This passage illustrates the strength of regional sentiment in the 1840s. Cattaneo's text became famous in anti-unification circles, and is much admired today by the separatist Northern League.

The Lombard plain is the most populous region in Europe. It has 176 inhabitants for every kilometre of surface, whereas the Belgian plain only supports 143 ... our people, by means of administrative institutions peculiar to ourselves, like rents fixed by law, local surtaxes and mutual obligations to maintain aqueducts, has so fertilised the land that on an area which provides in France for one family, we provide for two, while paying the same in taxes. Our rural municipalities have more schools; commerce and industry is linked intimately to all types of agriculture, so we have no hordes of industrial workers without firm roots in the land. Iron, silk, cotton, lino, leather and sugar are all objects of large-scale manufactures. The iron industry, spread around Como, Bergamo and Brescia, brings in eight million francs a year; Milan and Como have more than 8,000 silk looms, and 90,000 cotton spindles ... in 1840 there were 72 hospitals; another six were added in the next three years; seven more are being built; and they are open to all, simply on the basis of ill-health and need. The hospital of Milan alone takes in 24,000 patients a year; Paris, with a population four times the size, takes only three times as many. London takes as many as Milan: in proportion to population, we help ten people here to every one there. The poor are assisted by doctors, medicines and surgeons even at home, not only in the towns but in the most remote parts of the countryside. About half our doctors and surgeons, and three-quarters of our midwives, are paid by the municipalities to assist poor families ... this health army of doctors, surgeons, specialists, veterinary surgeons, midwives etc., amounts to just under 5,000 people. In the same way the country is supplied with engineers – in Milan alone there are about 450, whereas the Corps of Roads and Water in the whole of France only has 568; this greatly helps road-building and irrigation. The large number of educated people, in close and daily contact with the rest of the population, has a benevolent influence, helps to remove prejudice and inculcates a true sense of utility.

The large towns have 400,000 inhabitants, and there are many smaller towns with six, eight or ten thousand people each, which also contain numerous educated and prosperous families. Landownership is common among all classes. All things considered, this is probably the European country with the largest number of educated families in proportion to the illiterate poor ... without claiming to be better than other people, we can bear comparison with any other for intelligence and courage; and no other nation can compare with us for assiduous and persevering labour.

Carlo Cattaneo, Introduction to vol. 1 of *Notizie Naturali e Civili sulla Lombardia*, Milan, 1844; in C. Cattaneo, *Lombardia Antica e Moderna*, 1943 ed., Sansoni, Florence, pp. 97–101.

DOCUMENT 3   MAZZINI COMPLAINS OF BEING
MISUNDERSTOOD

By the early 1840s Giuseppe Mazzini had few supporters and little influence even among the revolutionaries. He was growing disillusioned, as these letters to fellow-conspirator Nicola Fabrizi, in Malta, show.

God forbid that I should add more bitterness to your burdens, but I do it almost as a justification for not being able to help you. When I wrote to you a long time ago, saying 'Alone, you can do nothing', do you think I meant to accuse you of not knowing what to do? No; I was accusing the Italians; between you and me, I do not respect them. I knew that they would promise money both to you and to me, but would not give any; that they would promise to act but would do nothing. Can't you see that they are prepared to be defeated one by one? Can't you see that if they were real men they would have acted *en masse*, at least in the Papal States, when Muratori was at the gates of Bologna with his armed band and the revolutionary ferment was widespread? Can't you see that they could have done so? I have known all this for ten years, long before this recent proof. I have no respect for my compatriots, and that is the greatest of my sorrows. The only way to rouse them is through hope, not idealism. You have to have money first, draw up a plan, tell them 'we are definitely going to act with our own resources at such and such a time; join us'. If we had all joined together, a real insurrection like that of 1831 in the Papal States was possible. But to get money beforehand, you need an organisation with a name, one that can create illusions and inspire confidence. This was the whole aim of my work with Young Italy abroad. And after a while I was succeeding, especially with the Americans and the English ...

If the rising doesn't occur now it's goodbye for centuries, or until such time as *la Grande Nation* sees fit to bring us our liberty. As for me, I will be discredited completely for having supported and helped your plan, and there will be nothing left for me but to write a curse on Italians of all parties – and I shall write it – and disappear from the scene. And I will do so. Apart from two or three individuals, I have no respect for my compatriots. The poor Irish are willing to give their last penny to an eloquent charlatan*; our lot wouldn't give a penny to avoid being clubbed by a German corporal. Upon my soul, which is finer than any of theirs, I am nauseated.

*Daniel O'Connell

Giuseppe Mazzini to Nicola Fabrizi, 30 November 1843, in G. Mazzini, *Epistolario*, xxiv [10, xlv], pp. 349–50; and 15 February 1844, in xxvi [10, xlviii], p. 67.

DOCUMENT 4   MASSIMO D'AZEGLIO, ARTIST, NOVELIST
AND POLITICIAN, RECALLS THE EARLY
1830s IN MILAN

And in truth, I ask you, is there nowadays an opinion, an idea, a thought, that cannot be freely uttered or printed in Italy, that cannot be freely discussed and deliberated upon? What absurdity, buffoonery or farce is there that cannot be presented to the respectable public in a hall, or on the stage of some second-rate theatre (of course, provided the hire be paid!), with its accompaniment of presidential bell, chairman and vice-chairman, orators, platform, german-silver candelabras, illuminations, &c.?

It is sufficient to respect the civil and criminal code; with that exception, you may assemble as much as you like, set forth your political, theological, social, artistic, literary theories; who on earth prevents you? Why then so many secrets? There is no escape from this dilemma; either it arises from folly, like that of children who act importance and ape their elders; or it is for the purpose of breaking the law and undermining the house in which we all live; or to give each other a helping-hand to secure good appointments, influence, or money, and thence oppose or support, not he who is useful or dangerous to the public, but he who counteracts or favours you in your intrigues. If this be all we have gained, we might as well have kept the Jesuits.

A free country has no need of mysteries; and in Italy, more than elsewhere, if we wish to disentangle ourselves quickly from our swaddling-clothes, we should carefully avoid everything that may lead to dissimulation or underhand practices.

This moral disease of ours offers the same phenomena as a great many epidemics. Take a country, for instance, where cholera is raging, all complaints degenerate into cholera; among us everything degenerates into a secret society.

That of *Giovine Italia* was a bad example and an evil school for Italy, from the absurdity of its political principles, the stupidity of its intentions, the perversity of its means, and lastly, on account of the mean behaviour of its leaders, who, while themselves in a place of perfect safety, sent to the scaffold the generous fools who did not understand that their heads were offered up not to regenerate Italy, but only to revive a withered sectarian zeal.

Yet even now there are people under the impression that our present liberty and independence are in great measure owing to these societies! It is true some also exist who hold that without the horrors of 1793, the world would not have been regenerated. They do not understand that terrorism, and the political sects which worked by assassinations and occult agencies, have inspired such horror, that, after so many years, men are only just beginning to be less frightened at liberty, and to prefer it to despotism.

Therefore all these infamies have not hastened, but, on the contrary, delayed our liberation.

During my stay at Milan, young men in general spent their time in drinking and running after ballet-girls (often marrying them); declaiming against the Austrians, keeping totally aloof from them; they were steeped in idleness and ignorance, and only a few bolder spirits took part in all the equally dark and useless proceedings of the *Giovine Italia*, which merely consisted in the circulation of letters, documents, newspapers, and pass-ports; assisting the flight of a secret agent, or such as were compromised; keeping up communications with prisoners, and the like. And to what purpose? They did not even know themselves, and I defy anybody else to tell.

Not sharing in the views of the *Giovine Italia*, knowing the perfect inutility of all the agitation in which its devotees indulged; and, moreover, detesting those habits of perpetual lying (not to speak of the daggers), I completely eschewed the whole thing. I was, and am still, of opinion that it is the national character which requires cultivation; that it is necessary to form the Italian mind, if we want Italy to be one nation; and when once it is formed, we shall indeed be able to say *Italia farà da sè*. Consequently I had devised a plan of acting on the public spirit by means of a national literature, and *Ettore Fieramosca* was the first step in that direction. In fact, during the whole period of my residence at Milan before 1845, the Austrian police had never occasion to interfere with me. If by chance they believed I was shrewd enough to baffle their vigilance, they would have laboured under a great mistake.

According to their ideas, I was strictly guiltless. It is true that I was preparing the means of attacking them in other ways, by which perhaps they were anything but gainers, and thus I have no claim on their gratitude.

M. d'Azeglio [42], ii, pp. 352–5.

DOCUMENT 5   **THE NAVY RELIES ON PATRIOTISM**

When war broke out in 1848, the Piedmontese Foreign Ministry ordered the navy not to fire on other ships.

It has not escaped the attention of the King's government that the majority of the officers and crews of the Austrian warships is made up of Italians; and that in a war which is essentially Italian, and aimed solely at driving the foreigners out of Italy, it would be a generous gesture not to fight against fellow-Italians. The Government has therefore requested the Admiralty to order the Commanders of royal warships to limit their activities to defending themselves if attacked by Austrian warships, without however provoking any engagement themselves.

Foreign Ministry to ship commanders, 31 March 1848; in Archivio di Stato di Cagliari, Real Secretario di Stato, b. 1701.

DOCUMENT 6   PIEDMONT MAKES OVERTURES TO
               FRANCE

In the autumn of 1848 Piedmontese diplomats, aware that Charles Albert
would probably renew the war against Austria in the spring, realized that
the French were reluctant to see Lombardy united with Piedmont. The
Piedmontese ambassador in London therefore tried to persuade his French
colleague otherwise, in a foretaste of Cavour's efforts that bore fruit at
Plombières a decade later.

[I told him that] as a result of our recent changes at home and of the war
which broke out in March, we have broken with Austria for good. A peace
treaty might re-establish an apparent harmony but it is obvious that this
harmony would only be apparent, and that conflict would be inevitable if
the peace gave us any part of the territories that had belonged to Austria. It
is not a question of likes or dislikes, but simply of real interests. Austria
would never give up hope of recovering the lost territory, and we would be
determined not to be deprived of it. Hence real antagonism, impossibility of
any alliance with Austria, and a pressing need for us to join closely with
France in order to avoid isolation. This seems to me so obvious that I do
not understand how anyone in Paris can have a different opinion. It is true
that Sardinia* would certainly increase her power by receiving Lombardy,
but this strength would be, so to speak, at the disposal of, and certainly to
the advantage of, France because it would make impossible any sincere
alliance between Sardinia and Austria, and would serve to make Piedmont a
stronger bulwark for France against any Austrian aggression.

M. de Beaumont agreed with me that this reasoning was correct, and
without admitting that his Government had a different opinion he assured
me that he had constantly attempted to show his Government that the
union of Lombardy with Piedmont was in the true interests of France.

*i.e. 'Kingdom of Sardinia', or Piedmont.

A. Di Revel, London, to Foreign Minister Perrone in Turin, 27 October
1848, in F. Curato and G. Giarrizzo [6], i, p. 320.

DOCUMENT 7   THE GRAND DUKE OF TUSCANY DECIDES
               ON WAR

In March 1848 Grand Duke Leopold of Tuscany was faced with a
dilemma: should he join Piedmont's war against the Austrians, who were
his own close relatives, or could he stay neutral?

My position was difficult and dangerous. I had to try and prevent Tuscany
falling into anarchy, which would have been fatal for Tuscany itself, a

dreadful example to the other states in Italy, and would have made the situation more difficult for everybody. Either I had to take part in the war, or go into exile and bring the government down. I had no desire to keep my throne, since ruling, which is always difficult, was at that time extremely difficult and dangerous. I had no ambition to enrich myself with other people's spoils. I had received no request to join my forces with those of the [Austrian] imperial army, as might have happened by treaty, and in any case this could not have been done: there was no way of moving them there. Nor did the Austrians offer their troops to Tuscany, so as to suppress the revolution; and I could not believe that Austria was in a position to send any troops. Tuscan neutrality was impossible too, in such a ferment.

I thought of my family links, and the dangers that my dynasty might incur if the situation changed; I thought of the anarchy that was imminent in Tuscany. I was the helmsman of a ship in a tempest, and my only thought was to save the ship and those who sailed in her. That evening, 29 March, I issued the decree which proclaimed war ... I had already granted a free press, a civic guard, and a Constitution; now I granted war. I intended to raise 2,000 conscripts, and nobody complained, not even about the extra cost, such was the popular enthusiasm.

Memoirs of Leopold II of Tuscany, in F. Pesendorfer (ed.) [11], pp. 333–4.

DOCUMENT 8   **RADETZKY'S REVENGE**

The Austrian commander in Lombardy, Field Marshal Radetzky, foretold the Milan rising; and, after his troops had crushed it, determined to stand no more nonsense.

It appears that the situation in Italy is regarded in Vienna as not sufficiently urgent to justify more than the usual security precautions. People forget, however, that we are dealing not with cabinets or the fickleness of princes or their ministers, but with a people that hate us and believe that the moment has come when it can finally throw off our yoke and can once again enter the ranks of great nations ... People forget that this nation has not yet sunk so low that it is incapable of a sudden resurgence. Great intellectual forces slumber in it. Napoleon was an Italian ... Italy may have declined but she also possesses the strength to rise again; and never was the feeling of her insignificance and the striving for national unity stronger and more universal in her than it is today. No statesman, no politician can foresee when and how the crisis which we face today will end.

... I am thoroughly convinced that it is high time to stop bestowing favours on a country which all too often abuses them; that it is much more necessary and imperative to let the country feel the punitive hand of its mighty and much offended lord, since everyone knows that the Italians fear a strict but just ruler and will do his bidding, while they abuse and despise a good and indulgent one.

In my opinion this wantonly wealthy land can only be punished most severely by the removal of those means which have seduced it into obstinacy and disobedience, for what is exile to the rich if they can take their money abroad and use it to create more trouble?

To humble the refractory rich, to protect the loyal citizen, but *in particular to exalt the poorer classes of the peasantry as in Galicia*, should be the principle on which from now on the government in Lombardy-Venetia should be based.

I am firmly convinced that directly after the conclusion of a peace or as things become absolutely hopeless for the revolutionary party, ringleaders like Casati and Borromeo and others, as well as the greatest part of those who have experienced punitive justice, will petition for clemency regarding their flight and that the government shall smother them in it. The aim of my present letter is, therefore, to beseech Your Excellency beforehand, to set aside any futile clemency and let justice run its course completely, that is, even with regard to the rich aristocracy and the larger cities, who have sinned so severely against the imperial, royal government.

Field Marshal Radetzky to Hardegg, 12 December 1847; Radetzky to Schwartzenberg, 13 April 1849; quoted in A. Sked [110], p. 103, p. 198.

DOCUMENT 9   THE MILANESE 'DEMOCRAT' GIORGIO PALLAVICINO CHANGES HIS MIND

Pallavicino, like many Lombard exiles in Turin after 1848, came to realise that Austrian rule could not be overthrown by popular revolt, but only by Piedmont. He was later the founder of the Italian National Society.

I, like you, believe that the life of a people lies in independence more than in liberty. But as an Italian first and foremost, I seek Italian forces for an Italian war, and a popular insurrection would not be enough for the purpose. We have seen this already: a popular rising can win temporary victories within the confines of its own cities, but without a miracle it cannot fight and defeat regular troops in the open countryside.

To defeat cannons and soldiers, you need cannons and soldiers of your own. You need arms, not Mazzinian chatter.

Piedmont has got soldiers and cannons; therefore I am a Piedmontese. Piedmont, by ancient custom, tradition, character and duty, is today a monarchy; therefore I am not a republican. And I am content with Charles Albert's Constitution. I anticipate that it will be improved in future, not so much by men's good will as by sheer necessity.

Independence, I repeat, is the very life of the nation. First independence, then liberty. First I want to live; I will think about living well later on.

I believe that a national war can only be fought with national weapons. Italy today possesses two strengths: Italian sentiment, and the Sardinian [Piedmontese] army. Each of these forces is impotent to act on its own; but the two together, the Sardinian army and popular insurrection, strengthen and reinforce each other, and we will soon easily have the armed Italy, that must necessarily precede a free Italy!

Pallavicino to General Pepe, 18 November 1851; in G. Pallavicino, *Memorie*, ii, Turin 1886, p. 438.

DOCUMENT 10   **THE EMPEROR NAPOLEON III PLANS THE FUTURE OF ITALY**

This note (of 22? March 1856) was written by Napoleon III as a memorandum for himself and his foreign minister. It reveals the Emperor's thinking, two years before Plombières.

The aim of all statesmen must be to avoid, as much as possible, all the ferments of dispute that still exist in Europe. Now one only has to open one's eyes to see that the country which is the greatest threat to European peace is Italy, because its political structure is such as not to satisfy any legitimate interest. To alter its structure either a revolution or a war is needed – two fatal extremities; and in any case who would be powerful enough to impose his will on so many divided countries, and which set of ideas would be accepted widely enough to unite so many States and give them a common purpose?

Nonetheless I believe that one might try something that might satisfy nearly everybody. An Italian Confederation might be set up, under the nominal leadership of the Pope, on the model of the German Confederation, i.e. a diet, appointed by the various States, could meet at Rome and discuss matters of common interest, without any change to territorial boundaries or to the rights of the various rulers.

Thus Austria, by reason of its Lombard territories, would be in the same position with regard to the Italian Confederation as is Holland now, with regard to the German Confederation.

This diet would not only deal with the major issues of general interest to Italy, such as tariffs, the army and navy, currency etc ... but it would have some administrative powers, and its decisions would be sovereign on matters of general interest. Each State would have one vote or representative for every one million inhabitants. Thus Piedmont would have five votes, of which one would be for Sardinia; Lombardy four votes; Tuscany one vote; Parma and Modena one vote; the Pope three votes: Naples four votes, of which one for Sicily. Total 18 votes.

Published in A. Saitta [12], i, pp. 81–2.

DOCUMENT 11 NAPOLEON III AND CAVOUR PLAN THE
WAR OF 1859

*The two men met at Plombières in July 1858. The first document cited is a
summary of the agreement they reached, written by Cavour's trusted aide,
Costantino Nigra. The second is Cavour's account of the meeting in a
subsequent letter to King Victor Emanuel.*

(a) Art. 1. Offensive and defensive alliance.

Art. 2. To cement this alliance, marriage.

Art. 3. In case of war breaking out in Italy between Sardinia [Piedmont] and
Austria, whether declared by Sardinia as a result of serious and just motives,
or by Austria, H.M. the Emperor of the French promises to come to the aid
of H.M. the King of Sardinia by placing an army corps and a fleet at his
disposal, as will be determined by a special convention.

Art. 4. Motives for a declaration of war against Austria would include
occupation by Austrian troops of any part of Italian territory except those
placed under occupation by the treaty of Vienna in 1815, violation by
Austria of existing treaties, and other motives of similar nature.

Art. 5. The French army corps mentioned above will be placed under the
command of H.M. the King of Sardinia. The Sardinian fleet will be joined
to that of France and placed under the orders of a French admiral.

Art. 6. Once war has begun, the High Contracting Parties undertake to
pursue it until Austrian troops have left Italian soil.

Art. 7. Territory conquered in Upper Italy and along the Po valley,
including Venice, the Duchies and the Legations, will be annexed to the
Kingdom of Sardinia, which will take the name of Kingdom of Upper Italy.

Art. 8. Once the Kingdom of Upper Italy has been formed, the population
of Savoy will be called upon to vote by universal suffrage on annexation of
the Duchy either to France or to Upper Italy.

Art. 9. Forbidden to negotiate separately. Equal treatment for plenipotentiaries of both sides in the peace congress.

(b) [The Emperor] began by saying he had decided to support Sardinia with
all his forces in a war against Austria, provided that the war was under-
taken for a non-revolutionary cause that could be justified in the eyes
of diplomacy and above all in that of public opinion in France and in
Europe ...

The search for a cause was the main difficulty to resolve before reaching
an agreement. At first I proposed to stress the problems that had arisen
because of Austria's failure to implement her commercial treaty with us. To
this the Emperor replied that a commercial question of minor importance
could not be the motive for a great war destined to alter the map of Europe.
I then proposed to raise once more the issues that had led us to protest at
the Congress of Paris against the illegitimate extension of Austrian power in

Italy, i.e. the treaty of 1847 between Austria and the Dukes of Parma and Modena, Austria's lengthy occupation of Romagna and the Legations, and the new fortifications she had built near Piacenza.

The Emperor did not accept this proposal. He observed that since these complaints had not been thought sufficient to bring about French or British intervention when we raised them in 1856, no-one would understand why they could justify going to war now. 'Moreover', he said, 'as long as my troops are in Rome, I can hardly demand that Austria withdraw hers from Ancona and Bologna'. The objection was reasonable. I therefore had to withdraw my second proposal, which I did reluctantly since it was bold and frank, and was perfectly suited to the noble and generous character of Your Majesty and of the people that you rule.

My position was becoming embarrassing, for I had nothing else to propose. The Emperor came to my aid and we went through all the states in Italy together, looking for a motive for war – and it was very difficult to find one. After travelling through the whole peninsula without success, we reached Massa and Carrara almost inadvertently, and there we discovered what we were looking for so keenly. I gave the Emperor an accurate description of that unfortunate region, although he had a fairly good idea of it already. We agreed that we would provoke an appeal by the inhabitants to Your Majesty for protection, and even a request for annexation of these Duchies to Sardinia. Your Majesty would not accept this proposal, but would take up the cause of this oppressed people and send the Duke of Modena a haughty and menacing note. The Duke, confident of Austrian support, would reply in an impertinent manner. Your Majesty would then occupy Massa and the war would begin.

Cavour to King Victor Emanuel, 24 July 1858, in [4], *Carteggio Cavour-Nigra*, i, pp. 101–04.

DOCUMENT 12   **KING VICTOR EMANUEL SPEAKS FROM THE THRONE**

The French and Piedmontese, preparing for war, made great efforts in early 1859 to provoke the Austrians. The following passage was suggested by Napoleon III for this purpose. It also made quite clear that Piedmont intended to go to war.

Fortified by our past experience, we go forward resolutely to whatever the future may hold. This future will be happy, for our policy rests on justice, love of liberty and love of our native country. Our State is small in territory but it has gained credit in the councils of Europe because it is great in the ideas it represents and in the friendship that it inspires. This situation is not without dangers. For while we respect treaties we are not insensitive to the cry of anguish that reaches us from so many parts of Italy. Strong in our unity, confident of the rightness of our cause, prudent yet determined, we await the decrees of divine Providence.

Speech of 10 January 1859, in O. Barie (ed.), *Le Origini dell'Italia Contemporanea*, Cappelli, Bologna, 1966, p. 23.

DOCUMENT 13   THE AUSTRIANS FALL INTO THE TRAP

The French chargé d'affaires in Vienna here reports to Paris why the Austrians decided on war.

As I have reported several times to Your Excellency, over-excited public opinion, encouraged by the army, has created here a domestic situation which is exercising so much pressure on the Government that it is perhaps impossible for it to resist even if it wished. In the ten years of his reign Emperor Francis Joseph has, on three different occasions, ordered general mobilization throughout his Empire: firstly against Prussia, secondly against Russia and now in the present circumstances. The first two times nothing happened except a futile threat of force, with the army receiving no benefit or reward from it. Today the Emperor is convinced that he cannot dismiss his troops again unless he obtains some real satisfaction from a despised enemy; to do so would show weakness, would lead to grave loss of authority for himself and would demoralise his army completely ...

[The Austrian Foreign Minister Count Buol told me] that he would refuse to admit plenipotentiaries of the Italian States [to a European congress on Italy], and he did not hesitate to declare that his refusal was caused by the Emperor's invincible repugnance to allowing his own plenipotentiary to sit at the same table as a Sardinian [Piedmontese] plenipotentiary, and that there was not a single Austrian who would forgive any minister who might advise in favour. 'We have shown our restraint', he said, 'in the face of constant Piedmontese provocation and insolence for three years now, patience and tolerance of which no other Great Power would have been capable, and certainly Emperor Napoleon would not have tolerated for three months from Belgium what we have had to put up with for three years from Sardinia'.

Banneville, French chargé d'affaires at Vienna, to French Foreign Minister Walewski, 20 and 21 April 1859, in A. Saitta [12], i, pp. 204–5.

DOCUMENT 14   THE BRITISH WORRY ABOUT FRENCH AGGRANDISEMENT

The British government was furious with Cavour in the spring of 1860 for ceding Nice and Savoy to France, and was determined to prevent France securing any more Italian territory. There were frequent rumours that Cavour intended to hand over Sardinia, and the British forced him to deny this publicly in parliament. On Cavour's death in 1861, the British put the same pressure on his successor Ricasoli.

a) The cession of Genoa to France would be utterly destructive of the independence of Italy. The cession of the island of Sardinia would be a serious derangement of the balance of power in the Mediterranean and it would be a deep stain on the King of Sardinia, if having bartered away the land that was the cradle of his Family [Savoy, ancestral home of the royal dynasty] he should give away the island which gives its name to his Monarchy, and in which during times of Italian adversity his ancestors found shelter and safety.

Memorandum of Lord Palmerston, Prime Minister, 22 May 1860; in Public Record Office FO 67:253 no.107.

b) It emerges from your despatch of 30 May no. 253 that French intrigues are on foot to get the island of Sardinia. Cavour often pronounced himself very strongly against any such measure; Her Majesty's Government is therefore desirous that you should state to Signor Ricasoli without delay that Cavour had denied to Her Majesty's Government any intention of ceding or bargaining away either the island of Sardinia, or any portion of Italian territory, and that Her Majesty's Government holds Signor Ricasoli bound to the same engagement as succeeding to the duties and functions of Count Cavour, and bound to fulfil the promises made by him to Great Britain on behalf of his royal master King Victor Emanuel.

You will state to Signor Ricasoli that this demand on the part of Her Majesty's Government implies nothing disadvantageous to the Kingdom of Italy, but the reverse; for while, on the one hand, Rome and Venetia are sure sooner or later to be added to the Italian Kingdom, and Rome probably sooner than Venetia; and while therefore there is no adequate reason for making any sacrifice of Italian interests to hasten the period at which either one or the other are to be added to the Kingdom; so on the other hand it must be obvious that the cession of the island of Sardinia, following upon that of Savoy and Nice, could be dishonouring to the King, would alienate from him and his Kingdom the sympathies of Europe and especially of England, would injuriously affect the balance of naval power in the Mediterranean to the detriment of the maritime Powers of Europe and especially of England; and while it deprived the Kingdom of Italy of a naval station and of a supply of shipbuilding timber, both of them of great value to Italy, it would place both in the hands of a Power which already occupied a commanding position as regards Italy. A glance at the map is sufficient to show the important bearing of Cagliari on Italian interests either as an Italian port or as the naval station of another Power.

You might add that the island of Sardinia has hitherto been greatly neglected by the Government of Turin, and that it would be good policy to conciliate the inhabitants of the island by introducing into it roads and bridges and the other arrangements of European civilisation.

Lord John Russell, Foreign Secretary, to the British Ambassador in Turin, Sir James Hudson, 10 June 1861; in PRO, FO 45:1, no. 119.

DOCUMENT 15   **GARIBALDI THE HERO**

This is one of several descriptions of Garibaldi by a follower and admirer. Giuseppe Bandi was one of the 'Thousand' who sailed with Garibaldi to Sicily in 1860.

Giuseppe Garibaldi at that time was nearer sixty than fifty years old. Those who had known him in America at the beginning of his adventurous career often told me that his character had not changed much over the years: always calm amid the greatest dangers, disposed to benevolence, moderate in good fortune and equanimous in adversity.

Quite a few men have been blessed by nature with the gifts of energy, courage and contempt for death, which shone forth from him; but very rarely, I think, have there been soldiers so serene and with such self-control as he. One might say, without fear of exaggeration, that the greater the danger, the more extraordinary the difficulty of the enterprise, the more clear and calm his eye became, and the more correct and perceptive his judgement ... he always had supreme confidence in himself and in his good fortune, and thus he was reluctant to ask advice from others, and contemptuous when advice was offered unasked.

He loved liberty and made himself her paladin; but he maintained that in the hour of danger it was necessary for all to obey the will of one individual. Some people said he had fallen in love with dictatorship when he saw how it operated successfully in the small republics of South America; but I believe he had, as it were, dictatorship in his bones, and that he had become convinced of the need for dictatorial rule because of the extraordinary campaigns he took up. Indeed, the major secret of his victories was his rapid, firm decision-making and the blind faith and devotion of his followers.

What often harmed Giuseppe Garibaldi was that he believed all men were honest, devoted to their country and free from any desire for personal gain; hence it often happened that if he heard accusations against someone who had wormed his way into his affections he would become indignant at what seemed to him malevolent slander, and his esteem for the accused would grow rather than diminish. And so he suffered much disillusionment, but he never learned to repent of his excessive trust, nor to recognise low cunning when he came across it ... he had no idea of the value of money, nor could he ever understand why most people prize it. He was very willing to forgive those who had offended him, but he was pitiless against the men who had ceded his native Nice to France. And every time he spoke of his native land, detached from Italy and handed over to the French Empire, he could not restrain his tears ...

No man can say he ever saw Giuseppe Garibaldi constrain his soldiers to obedience with threats or force; no man ever heard his voice raised in anger, except when he seemed to imitate the trumpet as he urged us on to attack. His universal reputation for justice, honesty and goodness formed a halo around his lion's head; the flash of his eyes or the sound of his voice, always calm and solemn, were enough to make the proud become obedient, the undisciplined become tame, the cowardly become brave. The man was so serene, so simple in his manners, his dress and habits; he had something so majestic, enchanting and attractive about him, that just to hear his voice you trembled and could not help loving him, and you would rush joyfully to face death under his gaze, as if it were a fine, divine thing to die observed and approved by such a man.

G. Bandi [16], pp. 371–6.

DOCUMENT 16   CAVOUR'S REACTION TO GARIBALDI'S SICILIAN EXPEDITION

On 16 May 1860 Cavour wrote to Ricasoli, telling him that Garibaldi had landed in Sicily.

It is great good fortune that he gave up the idea of attacking the Pope. He cannot be stopped from making war on the King of Naples. It may be good, it may be bad, but it was inevitable. If we had tried to restrain Garibaldi by force he would have become a real domestic problem. Now what will happen? It is impossible to predict. Will England help him? It is possible. Will France oppose him? I don't think so. And what about us? We cannot support him openly, nor can we encourage private efforts on his behalf. We have therefore decided not to allow any more sailings from Genoa or Livorno, but also not to prevent the despatch of arms and ammunition, provided they are sent off with a certain prudence. I fully recognise all the disadvantages of the ambiguous line that we are adopting, but I cannot work out any other policy that doesn't have even greater dangers.

Cavour to Ricasoli, 16 May 1860, in [4], *La Liberazione del Mezzogiorno e la Formazione del Regno d'Italia*, i, pp. 104–5.

Garibaldi's expedition to Sicily in 1860 fired immense enthusiasm abroad, particularly in Britain and the USA. Some volunteers set off to join him, and many people sent money for the cause. This cheque was sent by a group of Scottish 'Friends of Italy', and is signed by Garibaldi himself.

Cheque signed by Garibaldi. Archives of the Royal Bank of Scotland, Edinburgh; reproduced by kind permission of The Royal Bank of Scotland plc.

DOCUMENT 17   CAVOUR AND THE KINGDOM OF NAPLES

By late July 1860 Garibaldi controlled Sicily and was clearly intending to cross to the mainland in order to march on Rome. Cavour realized he could not allow Garibaldi to hold undisputed power in the south. Piedmont would have to move in, even if it meant renewed war with Austria.

If Garibaldi crosses to the mainland and takes over the Kingdom of Naples and its capital, as he has done in Sicily and Palermo, he becomes absolute master of the situation. King Victor Emanuel loses almost all his prestige; in the eyes of nearly all Italians, he becomes merely the friend of Garibaldi. He will probably keep his Crown, but the Crown will shine only with the reflected light emitted by a heroic adventurer. Garibaldi will not proclaim the republic at Naples, but he will not annex it to Piedmont either, and he will hold it as dictator. Once he has the resources of a kingdom of nine million inhabitants, as well as irresistible popular prestige, we cannot fight against him. He will be stronger than us. So what would be left for us to do? One thing only: join him, so as to make war against Austria together ... For a Prince of the House of Savoy it is better to perish in war than in revolution. A dynasty may rise again if it falls on the field of battle, but its fate is sealed for ever if it is dragged down into the mire.

Although we have decided what to do if Garibaldi is completely successful in the Kingdom of Naples, I believe it is our duty to the King and to Italy to do everything in our power to prevent his success. There is only one way to attain this result. We must ensure that the government in Naples falls before Garibaldi crosses to the mainland, or at least before he becomes master of it. Once the king of Naples has fled, we must take over government ourselves in the name of order and humanity, and seize the supreme leadership of the Italian movement from the hands of Garibaldi. This bold – you may prefer the word audacious – move will cause an outcry in Europe and will have serious diplomatic consequences, and may perhaps drag us eventually into war against Austria. But it saves us from revolution, and it preserves the true strength and glory of the Italian movement, its national, monarchical character.

Cavour to Nigra, 1 August 1860, in [4], *Carteggio Cavour-Nigra*, iv, pp. 122–3.

DOCUMENT 18   A 'DEMOCRAT' REFLECTS ON CAVOUR

In December 1860 rumours swept Italy that Cavour had died. The prominent Sardinian 'democratic' deputy Giorgio Asproni was not too displeased, as he confessed to his diary (5 December). In fact, Cavour lived on for another six months.

It is cowardice to rejoice at the fate that awaits all mortals, and for my part

I am indifferent to the loss of this statesman. His death, however, is providential for Italy. It will be extremely difficult, I should say impossible, for the moderate party to find anyone with the same combination of qualities to succeed him. He was from an aristocratic family, very rich, versatile, full of imagination, cunning and practised in the affairs of this world, quite unscrupulous, with no moral restraint, relaxed and courteous in his manner, but greedy and insatiable when it came to money or power. Wide-ranging in ideas, incomparable in intrigue, quick to grasp the point, blindly stubborn in his anger, he was determined to take any step, however dangerous, to defeat his opponents and maintain himself in office. He was lavish with banquets, jobs, decorations, handshakes, kind words, and secret service funds; he corrupted the electorate and the press, deceived public opinion and for ten years was complete master of the country. He has died now that his star looked like waning, and quite certainly he would have fallen in less than a year; but God knows what new evils he would have brought about in that period of omnipotence. He was small in stature, with a round face rather like Napoleon's, and reddish-white in complexion; fair hair, almost red, turning half-white in recent years; very large head, wide forehead, lively blue eyes, firm regular nose; his hair was becoming thinner and he was becoming half-bald. When he was still hoping to win me over politically, he was friendly and promised all kinds of good things for Sardinia. Once he found that I was firm in my principles, that I could neither be bought nor threatened and that my needs were few, he opposed me obstinately. He treated Sardinia as badly as he possibly could, and made a secret commitment to Louis Napoleon to cede it to France. Now he is no more; but the consequences of his stubborn war against revolution, which alone can bring independence, greatness and liberty to Italy, live on. The priests will say that he was struck down by the hand of God; perhaps they poisoned him. I say that he was a fortunate man both in life and in death, for a sudden end to life is a truly enviable stroke of good luck.

G. Asproni [2], ii, pp. 589–90.

DOCUMENT 19   GARIBALDI FAILS TO TAKE ROME

Garibaldi was not always successful, nor admired. In 1867, encouraged tacitly by the government, his volunteers invaded the remaining Papal territory, but were defeated at Mentana by Papal and French troops guarding the city. A German observer in Rome described events.

Whoever was in Rome at that time and witnessed these things, believed he had suddenly gone back to living in the Middle Ages, in a country where the rule of law was nil ... Garibaldi is outside the State, like a *condottiero*; he lives, a hermit agitator, on a lonely island*, far from the Italian mainland. He appears in his native land solely to carry out his military campaigns, regardless of the State, by means of popular agitations and bands of volunteers ... they hoped for an uprising in Rome, but that didn't take place. There was none in the States of the Church and least of all in Rome or Viterbo, where the agents of the revolutionary party had made efforts to provoke one. Only a real revolt, a clear expression of the popular will, could have justified intervention by Italy and absolutely ruled out any French support for the Pope. But since it didn't happen, and the population of the Roman state stayed calm, they tried in vain to pass off an invasion of volunteer troops from other regions as if it were a popular insurrection ... most of these bands were people jumbled together at random, many of them barely able to handle a gun. The sight of them would have sent a novelist or a romantic painter into raptures, but anyone with experience of war would have been dismayed. They were waiters, coachmen, servants, students, clerks, peasants, tailors, cobblers, artisans of all kinds, factory workers, all sorts of hungry jobless people. In their ranks there were also some well-educated men and youths, even some rich nobles, and also some emancipated women who followed the little army on horseback. Campaigns like this are found only in Italy, because only here is the strange character of the population suited to them. Certainly the main motives for all these people were need and the spirit of adventure, and it would be wrong to consider them simply as a gathering of rascals or rabble. They showed that patriotic fervour had spread from the democratic circles down to the lowest classes in society, and in fact these poor workers fought heroically at Mentana.

*Garibaldi had made his home on the island of Caprera, off north-east Sardinia.

F. Gregorovius, *Wanderjahre in Italien*, v, Leipzig, 1870–77, Italian translation Rome, 1906–9, iii, pp. 133–48.

DOCUMENT 20   **THE PIEDMONTESE ARMY ROOTS OUT BRIGANDS**

By the early months of 1861 the army was faced with widespread 'brigandage' in southern Italy. General Ferdinando Pinelli, in Ascoli, decided to encourage his troops. Note his attitude both to the local inhabitants and to the Church.

Officers and soldiers!
You have achieved a great deal already, but in war nothing has been achieved while something still remains to be done.

A troop of this brood of robbers is still hiding up in the hills. Root them out immediately, and be as merciless as fate.

Against such enemies pity is a crime. They are cowards: they will go on their knees before you when they see you in strength, but they will attack you treacherously from behind when they think you are weak, and massacre the wounded.

Indifferent to any political principles, greedy only for booty and looting, they are paid assassins; they may be currently employed by the Vicar not of Christ but of Satan, but they are ready to sell their daggers to others when the gold raised from the stupid credulity of the faithful is no longer enough to satisfy their lusts. We will annihilate them, and crush the Priestly vampire whose filthy lips have for centuries been sucking the blood of our Mother country. We shall purify with sword and fire the regions infested by its obscene slavering, and from the ashes liberty will arise in full vigour even in the noble province of Ascoli.

Major-General F. Pinelli, Proclamation to his troops, 3 February 1861, in A. De Jaco, *Il Brigantaggio Meridionale*, Riuniti, Rome, 1969, pp. 229–30.

GLOSSARY

capopopolo popular leader, particularly of urban artisans during insurrections.

Carbonari literally charcoal-burners, members of largest secret society in early nineteenth-century Italy.

'democrats' radical, often republican or revolutionary activists.

Legations provinces in the north of the Papal States administered by a cardinal-legate: Bologna, Ferrara, Ravenna and (after 1816) Forli and Pesaro. The number and boundaries of the Legations were frequently altered.

'moderates' advocates of constitutional liberalism, opposed to revolution and to secret societies.

Murattiani supporters of Napoleon I's brother-in-law King Joachim Murat of Naples (1808–15), or later (especially c. 1860) of the claims of his son Lucien to the throne of Naples.

'neo-ghibellines' advocates of an independent Italy under the leadership of a secular ruler. The Ghibellines were supporters of the medieval emperors against the papacy.

'neo-guelphs' advocates of an independent, federal Italy under the (formal) leadership of the Pope. The Guelphs were supporters of the papacy against the German emperors in the Middle Ages.

Orleanists constitutional monarchists in France, associated particularly with the rule of King Louis Philippe (1830–48), previously Duke of Orleans.

Quadrilateral the area bounded by the four fortress towns of Peschiera, Verona, Legnago and Mantua, on the borders of Lombardy and Venetia. The fortresses were normally held by Austrian troops.

Serenissima the Republic of Venice, abolished in 1797.

Sonderbund the coalition of Catholic cantons in Switzerland, losers in the civil war of 1847.

Temporal Power the Pope's role as ruler of the various Papal States in central Italy (as opposed to his ecclesiastical power as head of the Church, and his spiritual authority on matters of faith and morals). The nineteenth-century Church regarded the Temporal Power as essential, for otherwise the Pope would become the subject of a secular sovereign.

terraferma the mainland provinces of Venetia.

zelanti 'zealots', Catholic advocates of strong papal authority and centralisation in the Church, with no concessions to liberal or democratic ideals.

Zollverein customs league of German states founded in 1834. Austria was not a member.

CHRONOLOGY

1796   French troops led by Napoleon Bonaparte invade Italy and overthrow existing states.

1797   French set up Cisalpine Republic. Treaty of Campoformio between France and Austria: Republic of Venice dissolved and Venetia acquired by Austria.

1798   French set up Roman Republic.

1799   French set up Parthenopean Republic in Naples. Peasant revolt led by Cardinal Ruffo overthrows it. Austrian-led coalition defeats French troops, who leave Italy.

1800   Napoleon returns to Italy and defeats Austrians at Battle of Marengo (14 June). Restores Cisalpine Republic. Pius VII elected Pope.

1801   Austria and Naples make peace with France. French occupy Piedmont.

1802   Italian Republic (northern Italy) founded, with Napoleon as President. Piedmont annexed to France.

1804   Napoleon crowned Emperor by Pius VII.

1805   Italian Republic becomes Kingdom of Italy, with Napoleon as king, Beauharnais as viceroy. French law codes adopted. Liguria annexed to France. Austria loses battle of Austerlitz and cedes Venetia to Kingdom of Italy.

1806   French occupy Kingdom of Naples; Joseph Bonaparte becomes king. Feudalism abolished.

1808   French occupy Rome. French invade Spain and appoint Joseph Bonaparte as king; Joachim Murat becomes king of Naples.

1809   Papal States annexed to France. Pius VII imprisoned at Savona.

1812   Napoleon invades Russia, but is forced to retreat from Moscow. Constitution of British type promulgated in Sicily; more democratic one in non-occupied Spain.

1813   Napoleon loses battle of Leipzig and Coalition troops invade France (December).

1814   Napoleon abdicates. Kingdom of Italy collapses. Austria annexes Lombardy and Venetia; other former rulers restored, but Murat remains king of Naples.

1815   Napoleon escapes from Elba and resumes rule for 'Hundred Days', until defeated at battle of Waterloo. Austrians defeat

Murat and restore King Ferdinand IV of Naples. Congress of Vienna redraws map of Italy.

1816 Sicilian constitution and autonomy from Naples abolished. King Ferdinand becomes Ferdinand I of the Two Sicilies.

1818–19 Feudalism abolished in Sicily.

1820 Revolt in Spain triggers uprising in Naples. King Ferdinand promulgates Constitution. Revolt in Sicily, demanding independence from Naples and 1812 constitution, is put down by Neapolitan troops.

1821 Austria, Russia and Prussia meet at Ljubljana and decide to suppress constitutional regime in Naples. Austrian troops defeat Neapolitans and restore King Ferdinand. Revolt in Piedmont. King Victor Emanuel I abdicates. Charles Albert, acting as Regent, proclaims Spanish constitution, but is disowned by new king, Charles Felix. Piedmontese army suppresses revolt with Austrian backing.

1822 Greek revolt against Turkey. Austrian troops withdraw from Naples and Piedmont. Repression of 'constitutional' supporters in both states.

1823 Leo XII elected Pope.

1824 Ferdinand III, Grand Duke of Tuscany, dies and is succeeded by Leopold II.

1825 Ferdinand I of the Two Sicilies dies, succeeded by Francis I.

1829 Pius VIII elected Pope. Duchess of Massa-Carrara dies and territory incorporated into Duchy of Modena.

1830 Revolution in France triggers sporadic revolts in Italy. Francis I of Naples dies, succeeded by Ferdinand II. Pope Pius VIII dies (30 November).

1831 Gregory XVI elected Pope. Revolt in Modena spreads to Papal States. Austrian troops suppress it. Charles Felix of Piedmont dies and is succeeded by Charles Albert. Mazzini founds Young Italy.

1833 Mazzinian plot suppressed in Piedmont and elsewhere.

1834 Mazzinian insurrection at Genoa. Mazzinians also invade Savoy, unsuccessfully. Garibaldi, involved in Genoa plot, flees to South America.

1835 Emperor Francis I of Austria dies, succeeded by Ferdinand I.

1836 Feudalism abolished in Sardinia.

1839 First 'scientific congress' held at Pisa. First railway in Italy opened, from Naples to Portici.

1843 Gioberti's *Moral and Civil Primacy of the Italians* published in Brussels.

1844 Balbo's *The Hopes of Italy* published in Paris. Bandiera brothers lead unsuccessful insurrection in Calabria.

1845 Revolts in Emilia-Romagna.

1846   Duke Francis IV of Modena dies; he is succeeded by Francis V.
Pius IX elected Pope and grants amnesty to political prisoners.
Famine in many areas.

1847   Pius IX continues reforms, as do Leopold II in Tuscany and
Charles Albert in Piedmont. Lucca absorbed by Tuscany. Treaty
signed setting up Customs League between Papal States, Tuscany
and Piedmont.

1848   Rebels in Sicily set up their own government. Ferdinand II grants
constitution, as do Leopold II in Tuscany, Charles Albert in
Piedmont (the *Statuto*) and Pius IX. Tobacco strike in Lombardy
leads to anti-Austrian insurrection, the 'Five Days' of Milan;
Austrian troops withdraw from city. Charles Albert declares war
on Austria and invades Lombardy. Revolt in Venice proclaims
the Republic. Pius IX declares he cannot join war. Austrians
defeat Piedmontese at battle of Custoza, and retake Milan.
Ferdinand II resumes personal power in Naples and begins
reconquest of Sicily. Pellegrino Rossi assassinated in Rome; Pius
IX flees to Gaeta. Austrian Emperor Ferdinand I abdicates,
succeeded by Francis Joseph.

1849   Constituent Assembly in Rome proclaims Roman Republic and
the end of the Pope's Temporal Power. Leopold II flees from
Florence. Charles Albert resumes war against Austria and is
defeated again, at the battle of Novara. He abdicates and is
succeeded by King Victor Emanuel II. Leopold II returns to
Florence. French troops overthrow Roman Republic and restore
Pius IX. Republic of Venice surrenders to Austrians. D'Azeglio
becomes Prime Minister of Piedmont.

1850   Anticlerical laws passed in Piedmont. Cavour becomes Minister of
Agriculture.

1851   Cavour becomes Minister of Finance; makes commercial treaties
with neighbouring countries.

1852   Tuscan Constitution abolished. Cavour makes 'marriage'
(*connubio*) with centre-Left and in November becomes Prime
Minister of Piedmont.

1853   Mazzinian insurrection in Milan, suppressed.

1854   Duke Charles III of Parma assassinated; Maria Luisa de Bourbon
becomes Regent. Crimean War begins.

1855   Piedmont joins Crimean War and sends troops to Russia. Victory
at Chernaya Rechka.

1856   Cavour attends peace conference in Paris. Italian National Society
founded.

1857   Pisacane leads armed band to Sapri. Elections in Piedmont are
blow to Cavour.

1858   Orsini attempts to assassinate Napoleon III in Paris. Cavour and
Napoleon III meet at Plombières and agree on war against
Austria.

1859   King Ferdinand II of the Two Sicilies dies, and is succeeded by Francis II. Victory of Franco-Piedmontese alliance over Austria at battles of Magenta and Solferino. Duke Leopold II of Tuscany flees, as do Duke of Modena, Regent of Parma and Cardinal-Legate of Bologna. Pro-Piedmontese provisional governments set up in central Italy. Armistice of Villafranca leads Cavour to resign; replaced as Prime Minister by La Marmora. Lombardy is formally annexed by Piedmont.

1860   Cavour returns to power. Tuscany and Emilia vote in plebiscites for annexation by Piedmont. Savoy and Nice vote for annexation by France. Insurrection in Sicily triggers expedition of Garibaldi and the 'Thousand'. Garibaldi conquers Sicily in name of Victor Emanuel, then conquers Kingdom of Naples. Piedmontese troops take over Umbria and Marches, in Papal States, to prevent Garibaldi marching on Rome. Plebiscites ratify annexation of Sicily, Naples, Umbria and the Marches.

1861   First elections of Italian parliament. Victor Emanuel II proclaimed King of Italy. Death of Cavour. Parliament rejects regional devolution. Brigandage dominates in much of South.

1862   Garibaldi defeated at Aspromonte.

1864   Garibaldi makes triumphal visit to London. 'September Convention' between Italy and France on future of Rome. Riots in Turin.

1865   Capital of Italy moves from Turin to Florence.

1866   War between Italo-Prussian alliance and Austria gives Italy Venetia, despite lost battles of Custoza and Lissa. Anti-government rising in Palermo.

1867   Garibaldi again attempts to take Rome, but is defeated by French at battle of Mentana.

1869   Riots over grist-tax.

1870   Franco-Prussian War. French troops withdraw from Rome, and Italy takes city (20 September). Rome proclaimed capital of Italy.

BIBLIOGRAPHY

I have tried to restrict this bibliography to available works in English. The exceptions are when a work is cited in the text, or when an Italian work is so outstanding it simply has to be included. All books listed are published in London unless otherwise stated.

PRIMARY SOURCES

1   Abba, G.C., *The Diary of One of Garibaldi's Thousand*, Oxford UP, 1962.
2   Asproni, G., *Diario Politico 1855–76* (eds C. Sole and T. Orrù), 7 vols, Giuffrè, Milan, 1974–91.
3   Blakiston, N. (ed.), *The Roman Question. Extracts from the Despatches of Odo Russell from Rome 1858–70*, Chapman and Hall, 1962.
4   Cavour, C.B. di, *Carteggi di Camillo di Cavour*, 15 vols plus index, Zanichelli, Bologna, 1926–61.
5   Cavour, C.B. di, *Epistolario* (ed. C. Pischedda et al), 14 vols to date, Zanichelli, Bologna and Olschki, Florence, 1962– .
6   Curato, F. and Giarrizzo, G. (eds), *Le Relazioni Diplomatiche fra la Gran Bretagna e il Regno di Sardegna*, 3-a serie, 8 vols, Istituto Storico Italiano per l'Età Moderna e Contemporanea, Rome, 1961–9.
7   Mack Smith, D. (ed.), *The Making of Italy 1796–1870*, Harper and Row, New York, 1968.
8   Mack Smith, D. (ed.), *Garibaldi*, Prentice Hall, Englewood Cliffs, NJ, 1969.
9   Massari, G., *Diario dalle Cento Voci 1858–60* (ed. E. Morelli), Rocca San Casciano, 1959.
10 Mazzini, G., *Scritti Editi ed Inediti*, 106 vols, Imola, 1906–43.
11 Pesendorfer, F. (ed.), *Il Governo di Famiglia in Toscana. Memorie di Leopoldo II 1824–59*, Sansoni, Florence, 1987.
12 Saitta, A. (ed.), *La Guerra del 1859 nei Rapporti tra la Francia e L'Europa*, 3-a serie, 5 vols, Istituto Storico Italiano per L'Età Moderna e Contemporanea, Rome, 1960–2.
13 Woolf, S.J. (ed.), *The Italian Risorgimento*, Longman, 1969.

SECONDARY SOURCES

14 Absalom, R., *Italy Since 1800*, Longman, 1995.

15 Acton, H., *The Last Bourbons of Naples 1825–61*, Methuen, 1961.

16 Bandi, G., *I Mille da Genova a Capua*, Rizzoli, Milan, 1960 (1st ed. Salani, Florence, 1903).

17 Beales, D.E.D., *The Risorgimento and the Unification of Italy*, Longman, 1971, 2nd ed. 1981.

18 Beales, D.E.D., *England and Italy 1859–60*, Nelson, 1961.

19 Berengo, M., 'Le origini del Lombardo-Veneto', in *Rivista Storica Italiana*, lxxxiii (1971), 525–44.

20 Bizzocchi, R., *La Biblioteca Italiana e la Cultura della Restaurazione 1816–25*, Angeli, Milan, 1979.

21 Blumberg, A., *A Carefully-Planned Accident: the Italian War of 1859*, Associated UP, Toronto, 1990.

22 Broers, M., 'Italy and the Modern State: the experience of Napoleonic rule', in F. Furet and M. Ozouf (eds), *The French Revolution and the Creation of Modern Political Culture*, vol. 3, Pergamon, Oxford, 1989, 489–503.

23 Broers, M., 'Revolution and Risorgimento', in H.T. Mason and W. Doyle (eds), *The Impact of the French Revolution on European Consciousness*, Alan Sutton, 1989, 81–90.

24 Cafagna, L., 'The industrial revolution in Italy 1830–1914', in C. Cipolla (ed.), *The Fontana Economic History of Europe*, vol. 4, Fontana, 1973, 279–328.

25 Candeloro, G., *Storia dell' Italia Moderna., vols 1–5*, Feltrinelli, Milan, 1956–68.

26 Capra, C., *L'Età Rivoluzionaria e Napoleonica in Italia 1796–1815*, Loerscher, Turin, 1978.

27 Cattaneo, C., *Dell' Insurrezione di Milano nel 1848, e della Successiva Guerra*, Le Monnier, Florence, 1949 (1st ed. Amyot, Paris, 1848).

28 Cestaro, A., *Struttura Ecclesiastica e Società nel Mezzogiorno*, Ferraro, Naples, 1978.

29 Chabod, F., *Italian Foreign Policy: The Statecraft of the Founders*, Giovanni Agnelli Foundation, Princeton UP, NJ, 1996 (1st ed. Laterza, Bari, 1951).

30 Chadwick, O., *The Popes and European Revolution*, Oxford UP, 1981.

31 Cingari, G., *Mezzogiorno e Risorgimento*, Laterza, Bari and Rome, 1970.

32 Ciuffoletti, Z. and Rombai, L. (eds), *La Toscana dei Lorena*, Olschki, Florence, 1989.

33 Coppa, F.J. (ed.), *Studies in Modern Italian History*, Peter Lang, New York, 1986.

34 Coppa, F.J., *The Origins of the Italian Wars of Independence*, Longman, 1992.

35   Coppa, F.J., *Cardinal Antonelli and Papal Politics in European Affairs*, New York UP, Albany, NY, 1990.

36   Croce, B., *Storia d'Italia dal 1871 al 1915*, Laterza, Bari, 1927.

37   Davis, J.A., *Merchants, Monopolists and Contractors*, Arno, New York, 1981.

38   Davis, J.A., *Conflict and Control: Law and Order in Nineteenth-Century Italy*, Macmillan, 1988.

39   Davis, J.A., 'Remapping Italy's path to the twentieth century', in *Journal of Modern History*, lxvi (1994), 291–320.

40   Davis, J.A. (ed.), *Gramsci and Italy's Passive Revolution*, Croom Helm, 1979.

41   Davis, J.A. and Ginsborg, P. (eds), *Society and Politics in the Age of the Risorgimento*, Cambridge UP, 1991.

42   d'Azeglio, M., *Recollections*, 2 vols, Chapman and Hall, 1868 (1st ed. Florence, 1867).

43   della Peruta, F., *Mazzini e i Rivoluzionari Italiani*, Feltrinelli, Milan, 1974.

44   Duggan, C., *A Concise History of Italy*, Cambridge UP, 1994.

45   Forti Messina, A., 'I medici condotti e la professione del medico nell' Ottocento', in *Società e Storia* xxiii (1984), 101–61.

46   Galasso, G., *Mezzogiorno nella Storia d'Italia*, Le Monnier, Florence, 1984.

47   Ghisalberti, A.M. and Caracciolo, A. (eds), *L'Organizzazione dello Stato*, 11 vols, Giuffrè, Milan, 1960–6.

48   Gmarrizzo, G., *Mezzogiorno senza Meridionalismo*, Marsilio, Venice, 1992.

49   Ginsborg, P., *Daniel Manin and the Venetian Revolution of 1848–49*, Cambridge UP, 1979.

50   Gladstone, W.E., *Two Letters to the Earl of Aberdeen, on the State Persecutions of the Neapolitan Government*, London, 1851.

51   Gooch, J., *The Unification of Italy*, Methuen, 1986.

52   Gramsci, A., *Il Risorgimento*, Einaudi, Turin, 1949.

53   Greenfield, K.R., *Economics and Liberalism in the Risorgimento*, Johns Hopkins UP., Baltimore, Maryland, 1934, 2nd ed. 1965.

54   Grew, R., *A Sterner Plan for Italian Unity. The Italian National Society in the Risorgimento*, Princeton UP, NJ, 1963.

55   Grew, R., 'How success spoiled the Risorgimento', in *Journal of Modern History*, xxxiv (1962), 239–53.

56   Grew, R., 'Catholicism and the Risorgimento', in F.J. Coppa (ed.), *Studies in Modern Italian History* cit., 39–55.

57   Hales, E.E.Y., *Pio Nono*, Eyre and Spottiswoode, 1954.

58   Hales, E.E.Y., *Mazzini and the Secret Societies*, Eyre and Spottiswoode, 1956.

59   Hales, E.E.Y., *Revolution and Papacy 1769–1846*, Eyre and Spottiswoode, 1960.

60   Hancock, W.K., *Ricasoli and the Risorgimento in Tuscany*, Faber and Gwyer, 1926.

61 Hearder, H., *Italy in the Age of the Risorgimento*, Longman, 1983.

62 Hearder, H., *Cavour*, Longman, 1994.

63 Holt, E., *Risorgimento: the Making of Italy 1815–70*, Macmillan, 1970.

64 Hughes, S.C., *Crime, Disorder and the Risorgimento*, Cambridge UP, 1994.

65 Jemolo, A.C., *Church and State in Italy 1860–1960*, Blackwell, Oxford, 1960.

66 Johnston, R.M., *The Napoleonic Empire in Southern Italy and the Rise of Secret Societies*, 2 vols, Macmillan, Edinburgh, 1904.

67 Laven, D., 'Law and order in Habsburg Venetia', in *The Historical Journal*, xxxix (1996), 383–403.

68 Lo Romer, D., *Merchants and Reform in Livorno 1814–68*, California UP, Berkeley, Cal., 1988.

69 Lovett, C., *The Democratic Movement in Italy 1830–76*, Harvard UP, Cambridge, Mass., 1982.

70 Lovett, C., *Carlo Cattaneo and the Politics of the Risorgimento*, Nijhoff, The Hague, 1972.

71 Lyttelton, A., 'The national question in Italy', in M. Teich and R. Porter (eds), *The National Question in Europe in Historical Context*, Cambridge UP, 1993, 63–105.

72 Lyttelton, A., 'Shifting identities: nation, region and city', in C. Levy (ed.), *Italian Regionalism*, Berg, Oxford, 1996, 33–52.

73 Mack Smith, D., *Modern Sicily after 1713*, Cape, 1968.

74 Mack Smith, D., *Cavour and Garibaldi, 1860: a Study in Political Conflict*, Cambridge UP, 1954, 2nd ed. 1985.

75 Mack Smith, D., *Victor Emanuel, Cavour and the Risorgimento*, Oxford UP, 1971.

76 Mack Smith, D., *Cavour*, Methuen 1985.

77 Mack Smith, D., *Mazzini*, Yale UP, New Haven, Conn., 1994.

78 Mack Smith, D., *Italy and its Monarchy*, Yale UP, New Haven, Conn., 1989.

79 Macry, P., *Ottocento*, Einaudi, Turin, 1988.

80 Marshall, R., *Massimo d'Azeglio: an Artist in Politics*, Oxford UP, 1966.

81 Massafra, A. (ed.), *Il Mezzogiorno Preunitario*, Dedalo, Bari, 1988.

82 Meriggi, M., *Il Regno Lombardo-Veneto*. vol. 18, pt. 2, of *Storia d'Italia*, ed. G. Galasso, UTET, Turin, 1987.

83 Meriggi, M., *Amministrazione e Classi Sociali nel Lombardo-Veneto 1814–48*, Il Mulino, Bologna, 1983.

84 Meriggi, M., 'Società, istituzioni e ceti dirigenti', in G. Sabbatucci and V. Vidotto, *Storia d'Italia. Le Premesse dell' Unità*, Laterza, Bari and Rome, 1994, 119–228.

85 Meriggi, M., 'The Italian *borghesia*', in J. Kocka and A. Mitchell (eds), *Bourgeois Society in Nineteenth-century Europe*, Berg, Oxford, 1993, 423–38.

86 Miglio, G., *Io, Bossi e la Lega*, Mondadori, Milan, 1994.
87 Morley, J., *The Life of Gladstone*, 2 vols, Lloyd, 1908.
88 Nada, N., *Dallo Stato Assoluto allo Stato Costituzionale*, Istituto della Storia del Risorgimento Italiano, Turin, 1980.
89 Petrusewicz, M., *Latifondo. Economia Morale e Vita Materiale in una Periferia dell' Ottocento*, Marsilio, Venice, 1989.
90 Petrusewicz, M., 'Society against the State: peasant brigandage in Southern Italy', in *Criminal Justice History*, viii (1987), 1–20.
91 Raponi, N. (ed.), *Dagli Stati Preunitari d'Antico Regime all' Unificazione*, Il Mulino, Bologna, 1981.
92 Rath, R.J., 'The *Carbonari*: their origins, initiation rites and aims', in *American Historical Review*, lxix (1964), 353–70.
93 Rath, R.J., *The Provisional Austrian Regime in Lombardy-Venetia 1814–15*, Texas UP, Austin, Texas, 1969.
94 Reinerman, A.J., *Austria and the Papacy in the Age of Metternich*, 2 vols, Catholic University of America, Washington, DC, 1979–89.
95 Reinerman, A.J., 'The failure of popular counter-revolution in Risorgimento Italy: the case of the *centurioni*', in *The Historical Journal*, xxxiv (1991), 21–41.
96 Reinerman, A., 'Metternich, Italy and the Congress of Verona 1821–22', in *The Historical Journal*, xiv (1971), 262–87.
97 Riall, L.J., *The Italian Risorgimento. State, Society and National Unification*, Routledge, 1994.
98 Riall, L.J., 'Elite resistance to State formation', in M. Fulbrook (ed.), *National Histories and European History*, UCL Press, 1993.
99 Ridley, J., *Garibaldi*, Constable, 1974.
100 Roberts, J.M., *The Mythology of the Secret Societies*, Secker and Warburg, 1972.
101 Robinson, J.M., *Cardinal Consalvi*, Bodley Head, 1987.
102 Romanelli, R., *Il Comando Impossibile*, Einaudi, Bologna, 1988.
103 Romanelli, R., 'Political debate, social history and the Italian bourgeoisie', in *Journal of Modern History*, lxiii (1991), 717–39.
104 Romani, M., *Storia Economica d'Italia nel Secolo XIX*, Il Mulino, Bologna, 1982.
105 Romeo, R., *Cavour e il suo Tempo*, 3 vols, Laterza, Bari and Rome, 1969–84.
106 Rosselli, J., *Lord William Bentinck and the British Occupation of Sicily 1811–14*, Cambridge UP, 1956.
107 Sabbatucci, G. and Vidotto, V., *Storia d'Italia. Le Premesse dell' Unità*, Laterza, Bari and Rome, 1994.
108 Scirocco, A., *L'Italia del Risorgimento 1800–60*, Il Mulino, Bologna, 1990.
109 Sked, A., *Decline and Fall of the Habsburg Empire 1815–1918*, Longman, 1989.
110 Sked, A., *The Survival of the Habsburg Empire*, Longman, 1979.
111 Sperber, J., *The European Revolutions 1848–51*, Cambridge UP, 1994.